This book is backed by latest research findings.

ISBN 978-0-9995575-4-9
Library of Congress
Book designed and illustrated by Stephanie Fernandez

Executive Editor Danielle Houck

Authors: Kay Lopate and Patsy Self Trand

Published independently by Pinecrest Street Company, Inc.
Address 11301 S. Dixie Hwy. Box 566684 Miami FL 33156
Printed in the United States

Researched and written by Kay Lopate, Ph.D. Patsy Self Trand, Ph.D.

PINECREST STREET CO. PUBLISHING

30

Amazing

READING
AND
LEARNING
STRATEGIES
FOR COLLEGE
STUDENTS

EIGHT BONUS STRATEGIES INCLUDED!

WRITTEN BY   KAY LOPATE, PH.D.   PATSY SELF TRAND, PH.D.

Books Published by Pinecrest Street Company, Inc.

Taking on the Challenge Series:

Making it to Graduation: Expert advice from college professors.
(2017). Lopate, Kay and Trand, Patsy Self. Pinecrest Street
Company, Inc.

The Official Parent Playbook: Getting your child through college.
(2017) Lopate, Kay and Trand, Patsy Self. Pinecrest Street Company,
Inc.

Making it in Medical School: Expert advice from college professors.
(2018). Lopate, Kay and Trand, Patsy Self. Pinecrest Street
Company, Inc.

Making it in Nursing School: Expert advice from college professors.
(2018). Trand, Patsy Self, and Lopate, Kay. Pinecrest Street
Company, Inc.

The Athletes' Playbook for College Success. (2018). Trand, Patsy
Self and Lopate, Kay. Pinecrest Street Company, Inc.

Vocabulary University Professors say all College Students Should Know. (2017).
Trand, Patsy Self and Lopate, Kay. Pinecrest Street Company, Inc.

College Bound Series

30 Awesome Reading and Learning Strategies for High School Students. (2018.) Trand, Patsy Self and Lopate, Kay. Pinecrest Street Company, Inc.

Become a Great Reader and Writer in College. Book 1. (2017). Lopate, Kay and Trand, Patsy Self. Pinecrest Street Company, Inc.

Getting the Basics of Critical Thinking for College Readers and Writers. Book 2. (2018) Lopate, Kay and Trand, Patsy Self. Pinecrest Street Company, Inc.

Reading and Learning the Required College Courses in the Historical and Social Sciences. Book 3. (2017). Trand, Patsy Self and Lopate, Kay. Pinecrest Street Company, Inc.

Reading and Learning the Required College Courses in the Biological and Mathematical Sciences. Book 4 (2017). Trand, Patsy Self and Lopate, Kay. Pinecrest Street Company, Inc.

Navigating Through College Series

30 Amazing Reading and Learning Strategies for College Students. (2017). Lopate, Kay and Trand, Patsy Self. Pinecrest Street Company, Inc.

Why I Didn't Come to Class. (2018). Trand, Patsy Self and Lopate, Kay. Pinecrest Street Company, Inc.

Capturing the Experience: My Child's First Year in College. (2018) Carpenter, Sara, Lopate, Kay and Trand, Patsy Self. Pinecrest Street Company, Inc.

Capturing the Experience: My First Year in College. (2018). Carpenter, Sara, Lopate, Kay and Trand, Patsy Self. Pinecrest Street Company, Inc.

PINECRESTSTREETCO.
PUBLISHING

30 Amazing Reading and Learning Strategies for College Students

The book that every college student should have!

Forward

What makes this book so amazing?

Most students prepare for their exams and classes by doing the same thing: reading and rereading their class notes and superficially reading the textbook without fully comprehending the subject matter. They fail to realize that because each assignment is different, a different strategy or plan of action is needed.

In the same way a successful businessperson has detailed plans for each task, a successful college student needs a suitable strategy for every important assignment. Simply put, as course work changes, so should the strategy. "Thirty Amazing Reading and Learning Strategies for College Students" focuses on finding the right "GPS"—"Getting the Perfect Strategy", and we instruct our students when and how to implement the perfect learning strategy depending on the assignment at hand.

New technologies not only impact our knowledge base, but also the way we learn. The best students should be flexible and be prepared to pivot from one learning strategy to the next for optimal learning. This is the purpose of this book—to introduce students with the reading and learning strategies we have found to be successful in helping them achieve their goals. What makes this book so amazing is that while students are acquiring a repertoire of reading and learning strategies, they are also strengthening their reading comprehension abilities.

Features of Thirty Amazing Reading and Learning Strategies

- Suggests strategies to use with courses
- Describes the goal of the strategy
- Can be used individually or with groups
- Can be used by students in all majors
- Students are actively involved
- Lists the materials needed
- Includes student comments
- Includes instructor comments
- States the amount of time needed to complete the strategy
- Describes in a paragraph why students need to learn the strategy
- Provides directions for "Getting Ready for the Activity"
- Provides directions for "The Activity"
- Has Home Learning "tips"
- Has "Learning Hint" (extension of strategy)
- Includes a "GPS", "Getting the Perfect Strategy", which matches the assignment with a strategy
- Includes a "Crosswalk" to match a course with a strategy
- Has a "finished product" that can be graded.

The strategies are the result of years teaching college students. We believe the strategies were instrumental in helping all students become "better students". Most of the 30 strategies are "original" (you won't find them anywhere else) although we included some that have been around awhile!

We recommend students become familiar with all the strategies; however, we recommend that students choose 4-5 strategies that relate to their classes and become proficient in them.

We are including 8 bonus strategies for Math and English, the two areas that are documented as the most problematic for college students.

Table of Contents

1   All Modalities..7

2   Alternate Sources..10

3   Annotation...13

4   Applicable Apps...15

5   Back Pack..18

6   Beating the Nods..20

7   Bold to Bold..22

8   Book of Mistakes..24

9   Cover It Up, Then Read..26

10   Crossword Puzzle Maker...28

11   Dictionary, Check It...30

12   Five Minute Summary with Laptop.....................................32

13   Friend to Friend...34

14   How to Deal with Professors...36

15   Legal Cheat Sheet..39

16   Lock Screen...41

17   Make a Test..44

18   My To Do List..46

19   Once Upon a Time...48

20   Pace Reading...51

21 Powerful Power Points..53

22 Rap..55

23 Say It, Then Play It..57

24 Sketch Book Journal..59

25 SQ3R Modified for College..61

26 Summertime Smarts..64

27 Twenty Most Important Things..66

28 Take Apart Notebook..68

29 Teach It...70

30 Visual-Text Connection..72

Bonus Chapter- Strategies Specific for Mathematics and English............74

Mathematics

1.   Back –up System Modified for Mathematics.........................75

2.   Bank Deposits..77

3.   Camera Roll...80

4.   Validity Web..82

English

1.   Check the Facts...88

2.   Patterns for Organization..90

3.   Transitions and Prepositions...95

4.   Writing Around the Table..105

Curriculum Core- The required courses, regardless of major, during the first two years of college/university

CURRICULUM CORE AND STRATEGY CROSSWALK

Historical Sciences	English Composition and Literature	Natural Sciences
➤ Sketch Book Journal	➤ Alternate Sources	➤ Outline by Heading
➤ Once Upon a Time	➤ 20 Most Important Things	➤ Bold to Bold
➤ Bold to Bold	➤ 5 Minute Summary for Laptop Users	➤ Sketch Book Journal
➤ SQ3R Modified for College	➤ Writing Around the Table	➤Visual Text Connection (VTC)
➤ Alternate Sources	➤ Pace Reading	➤ Annotation
➤ Annotation	➤ Sketch Book Journal	➤ Applicable Apps
➤ Applicable Apps	➤ Transitions/Prepositions	➤ Back Pack
➤ Back Pack	➤ Patterns for Organization	➤ Beating the Nods
➤ Beating the Nods	➤ Fact Check	➤ Dictionary, Check It
➤ Dictionary, Check It	➤ Crossword Puzzle Maker	➤ Legal Cheat Sheet
➤ Legal Cheat Sheet	➤ Cover It Up, Then Read	➤ Lock Screen
➤ Lock Screen	➤ RAP	➤ Make a Test
➤ Make a Test	➤ Summertime Smarts	➤ Once Upon a Time
➤ Powerful Power Points		➤ Teach It

Humanities	Mathematics and Statistics	Social Inquiry
➤ Friend to Friend	➤ Pace Reading	➤ Bold to Bold
➤ Alternate Sources	➤ Camera Roll	➤ Say It, Then Play It
➤ Powerful Power Points	➤ Banking Deposits	➤ All Modalities
➤ Make A Test	➤ Validity Web	➤ Applicable Apps
➤ See It, Then Play It	➤ Backup System for Mathematics	➤ Back Pack
➤ All Modalities	➤ Back Pack	➤ Beating the Nods
➤ Crossword Puzzle Maker	➤ Book of Mistakes	➤ How to Deal with Professors
➤ Cover It Up, Then Read	➤ Lock Screen	➤ Once Upon A Time
➤ How to Deal with Professors	➤ Make a Test	➤ SQ3R Modified for College
➤ RAP	➤ Teach It	
➤ Summertime Smarts		
➤ 20 Most Important Things		

Arts	First Year Experience	Physical Sciences
➤ Sketch Book Journal	➤ Five Minute Summary for Laptop Users	➤ Friend to Friend
➤ Mapping	➤ All Modalities	➤ Legal Cheat Sheet
➤ All Modalities	➤ Transitions/Prepositions	➤ Studying on the Run
➤ Applicable Apps	➤ Patterns for Organization	➤ SQ3R Modified for College
➤ Book of Mistakes	➤ 20 Most Important Things	➤ Back Pack
➤ Crossword Puzzle Maker	➤ Alternate Sources	➤ Beating the Nods
➤ Visual Text Connection (VTC)	➤ Crossword Puzzle Maker	➤Visual Text Connection (VTC)
➤ My To Do List	➤ How to Deal with Professors	➤ Once Upon A Time
➤ Pace Reading	➤ My To Do List	➤ Pace Reading
➤ RAP	➤ Summertime Smarts	➤ Powerful Power Points
➤ Say It, Then Play It		➤ Teach It

Legend

Historical Sciences- History courses

English Composition and Literature- English writing courses and Literature
Courses

Natural Sciences- Biology, Chemistry, Physics

Humanities- Philosophical Analysis, World Civilization

Mathematics and Statistics- Finite Math, Algebra, Calculus, Trigonometry,
Statistics,

Social Inquiry- Psychology, Human Growth and Development

Art- Art History, History of Art

First Year Experience- Freshman Experience

Physical Sciences- Earth Science, Astronomy, Environmental Studies

GPS | Getting the Perfect Strategy

Use the GPS to find the perfect strategy for each assignment!

If your textbook has a lot of illustrations	**Sketch Book Journal, VTC-Visual-Text-Connection, Lock Screen**
If your text has wide margins or bold headings	**Annotation, Bold to Bold**
If you like using an iPhone use	**Back Pack, Lock Screen, Say It, Then Play It, Applicable Apps**
If you like being creative when studying	**Once Upon a Time, Sketch Book Journal, Rap**
If the material is especially boring	**Five Minute Summary with Laptop, Once Upon a Time, Friend to Friend, "Say It, Then Play It", Sketch Book Journal, Beating the Nods**
If most of the vocabulary is new to you	**Crossword Puzzle Maker, Dictionary Check It**
If you have very little background knowledge	**Alternate Sources**
If you are going to have an essay exam	**Annotation, Back Pack, Teach It**
If you are easily distracted or have a short attention span	**My To-Do List, Teach It, Make A Test, Five Minute Summary with Technology, Applicable Apps**
If you are working with a group or study partner	**Back Pack, Rap, Friend to Friend**
If you have a lot of information to read in a short amount of time	**Say It, Then Play It**

If the textbook is too difficult for you	**All Modalities, Alternate Sources, Bold to Bold, Say It, Then Play It, Cover It Up, Then Read, Lock Screen**
If you need to study for a test	**Back Pack, Legal Cheat Sheet, Banking Deposit, Make a Test, Twenty Most Important Things**
If you want a head start in class	**My To-Do-List, Alternate Sources, Summertime Smarts**
If you like to take notes on a laptop	**Five Minute Summary with Laptop**
If you have trouble with reading comprehension	**Cover It Up, Then Read, Once Upon a Time, SQ3R, Alternate Sources, Pace Reading, Twenty Most Important Things**
If you have trouble with organization	**My To-Do-List, Bold to Bold, Powerful Power Points, Take Apart Notebook**
If you have trouble remembering information	**Book of Mistakes, Rap, Crossword Puzzle Maker, Twenty Most Important Things, Legal Cheat Sheet, Sketch Book Journal, Make A Test**
If you want to impress your teacher	**Beating the Nods, How to Deal with Professors, Teach It**
If you find math problems difficult	**Bank Deposits, Lock Screen, Back-Up**

1 | All Modalities

Course	U.S. History, U.S. Government, World History / Civilization, Economics, Geography, English Composition, Literature, Biology, Chemistry, Earth Science, Life Science, Physics, Physical Education, Health, Discrete Math, Algebra, Geometry, Calculus, Trigonometry, Statistics, Foreign Language, Art History, Art Appreciation, Online Courses, Career Education
Goal	To increase learning by using more modalities (listening, reading, speaking, and writing)
Materials needed	Class notes, textbook, recording device, paper and pencil
Student comments	*"I like to record myself reading the textbook because I can lie on my bed and listen. Sometimes reading can be boring. I also like pretending I'm the teacher and teach mini lectures!"*
Professor comments	*"Too often students only use the visual or auditory modality. I like the strategy because it includes the kinesthetic mode and writing ."*
Lesson duration	50 minutes to one hour
Finished product to be graded	Volunteer to give your "ten minute mini-lecture" to the class and turn for a grade in the summaries of the most important topics.

Why do I need to learn this?

Most of the time people acquire information by reading or by listening. Typically, students read their textbook and then listen to their teacher's explanation. Another modality that is used less often is the kinesthetic modality. This modality includes writing about the topic or teaching the material to someone. So, if you want to increase learning, we suggest that you use all three modalities.

Getting Ready for the Activity

1. For an upcoming test select the textbook chapters, class notes, and other information that will be covered.

The Activity

2. Skim through all textbook chapters, class notes, and other information and with a pencil, mark the most important information.
3. Read aloud the important information you marked in pencil into a recording device.
4. Play back the recording and listen to everything you recorded.
5. Use class notes and any other information that might be on the test and prepare a 10 minute "mini-lecture". Use a whiteboard to explain the information.
6. Write 4-6 summaries for the most important topics.
7. Review by listening to your recordings and reviewing the "mini-lectures" and summaries.

Home Learning

Remind students that learning is intensified when several modalities are used.

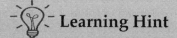 **Learning Hint**

Using more than one modality will deepen and increase learning. Too often students only use one modality. Remind students that the best way to learn something is to teach it to someone else.

2 | Alternate Sources

Course	U.S. History, U.S. Government, World History / Civilization, Economics, Geography, English Composition, Literature, Biology, Chemistry, Earth Science, Life Science, Physics, Physical Education, Health,Discrete Math, Algebra, Geometry, Calculus, Trigonometry, Statistics, Foreign Language, Art History, Art Appreciation, Online Courses, Career Education
Goal	To learn information from additional resources
Materials needed	Additional resources such as internet, library sources, other textbooks, newspapers, journals, and encyclopedias
Student comments	*"Learning became easier when I was able to use other sources. The textbook was too difficult for me, so I was able to learn what I needed to know from an online encyclopedia.*
Professor comments	*"Alternate Sources encourages students to use many resources—this is a strategy that all students need to develop."*
Lesson Duration	Time will vary.
Finished product to be graded	Meet with your professor during office hours to hand in the list of alternate sources used. During this meeting give an evaluation of the most helpful resources.

Why do I need to learn this?

There will be times in college when you won't understand something. This can be serious especially when several weeks go by and you still don't understand. For example, in psychology you may have to learn about Sigmund Freud's defense mechanisms. Although your professor explained these and you have read about them, you still don't know them well enough.

Alternate Sources Strategy is an easy way to get another explanation on the same topic. Some resources available might be the internet, library books, tutoring center, your professor, study guides from the publisher, reference librarian, and other textbooks. Remember, that since your goal is to increase understanding, it is quite possible that another writer explained the concept in a more comprehensible way.

Getting Ready for the Activity

1. Identify the material that you do not understand.
2. Make an appointment with your professor, student learning center, and the media specialist or reference librarian.

The Activity

3. Be prepared to talk to your professor about your concerns regarding the problems you have learned in class. Ask the professor to recommend some alternative sources and the best way to use them.
4. Meet with the media specialist or reference librarian to locate and recommend the alternate sources related to your topic.
5. Find additional sources from the internet and print relevant articles.
6. If possible, check out several books on the subject. If you use reference material that can't be checked out, either take notes or copy relevant pages.

7. Read your alternate sources, then reread class notes, and reread your assigned textbook. Make a list of all references used and also make a list of questions and/or concepts that need clarification.

8. If some topics are still unclear, ask questions in class, get tutoring help, or see your professor during office hours. Let your professor know that you followed his/her advice and ask if there is anything else that you might do to make a good grade in the class.

9. Meet with your professor, show the list of alternate sources, and discuss/ evaluate all the alternate sources.

Home Learning

Keep your notes from alternate sources with your class notes for easy retrieval. As you study, write questions that you think the professor might ask on the next test.

Learning Hint

Jerome Bruner, a prominent cognitive psychologist, said that everyone is capable of learning anything as long as instruction is at an appropriate level. Since there is a wide variety among individuals in their learning styles and abilities, not everyone may be able to learn from the same materials. It really does not matter what materials you use—it only matters that you learned what you intended to learn! Take the initiative and always have a few alternative sources available when you study!

---

3 | Annotation

Course	U.S. History, U.S. Government, World History / Civilization, Economics, Geography, Biology, Chemistry, Earth Science, Life Science, Physics, Health, Career Education
Goal	To increase learning from textbooks
Materials needed	Textbook, pen, pencil, highlighters
Student comments	*"Annotation takes a long time but it helps me concentrate. I'm trying to annotate at least five pages in every chapter."*
Professor comments	*"One of the main reasons why students have trouble comprehending is because they can't concentrate. Their minds wander and lose attention. Annotation is the best strategy for engaging students with the textbook—when they begin to focus, comprehension improves."*
Lesson duration	Time will vary
Finished product to be graded	Show the annotated pages to the instructor.

Why do I need to learn this?

A problem many students have with reading comprehension is that their minds wander. They lose concentration and little, if anything, is learned. Annotation is one of the best reading comprehension strategies because it practically guarantees complete understanding! Annotation takes more time than other comprehension strategies, so we suggest that you only annotate 4-5 pages per chapter. You can use other strategies for the rest of the chapter unless you have time to annotate everything.

Getting Ready for the Activity

1. Choose a textbook reading assignment from one of your classes. Make sure the pages in the textbook have wide margins.

The Activity

2. Begin by reading a complete paragraph.
3. After you have read the paragraph, ask yourself, "What is the main idea?"
4. Write the main idea in the margin.
5. With your pencil mark anything in the paragraph that might be important such as definitions, terms, names, numbers, dates, information in quotes, or examples using stars, underlining, circles, brackets, and arrows. Also use space in the margin to add anything you think is important.
6. Review your marginal notes and markings you made within the text. Use different color highlighters. Review annotations several times before a test.
7. Repeat until 4-5 pages are annotated.

Home Learning

You can annotate any kind of informational text. Practice annotating newspaper articles and magazines.

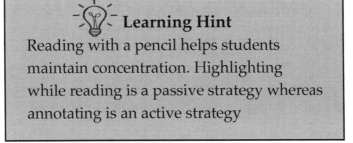

Learning Hint

Reading with a pencil helps students maintain concentration. Highlighting while reading is a passive strategy whereas annotating is an active strategy

4 | Applicable Apps

Course	U.S. History, U.S. Government, World History / Civilization, Economics, Geography, English Composition, Literature, Biology, Chemistry, Earth Science, Life Science, Physics, Physical Education, Health, ROTC, Discrete Math, Algebra, Geometry, Calculus, Trigonometry, Statistics, Foreign Language, Art History, Art Appreciation, Band, Music, Online Courses, Career Education
Goal	To increase learning by using apps
Materials needed	Mobile devices, apps, textbook, class notes
Student comments	*"I started using iStudiezLite app and it has kept me on track with all my courses. But the most amazing app is Mathway. I used to hate math and now I like it a lot more."*
Professor comments	*"It's a good idea for students to become familiar with apps that relate to their courses. I spend part of one class each semester introducing the students to apps that are sure to make a difference!"*
Lesson duration	Time will vary.
Finished product to be graded	3-5 minute presentation of topic

Why do I need to learn this?

Apps are changing the way people learn and, without a doubt, are enhancing education. They are affordable, easy to understand, usually entertaining and motivating, and available 24/7. This strategy is a good introduction that makes college students seek ones that are designed for their classes.

Getting Ready for the Activity

1. Make a list of apps you would like to know about. The 15 apps listed below correspond to college courses. You may choose different apps to fit the requirements of your course.

a. Brainscape: Brainscape has online flashcards or allows you to create your own. Learning is optimized through spaced learning, repetition, use of color, font styles, sounds, and humor.

b. Coursera: Coursera supplements knowledge with access to the world's top universities and lecturers. It provides instruction to anyone wherever they may be.

c. Dictionary.com: Dictionary.com is a #1 award free dictionary for mobile devices with over two million definitions.

d. Duolingo: Duolingo is a fun way to learn a new language. Each lesson includes speaking, listening, translating, and instant feedback of correct and incorrect answers.

e. DragonDictation: DragonDictation converts speech into words. It also allows you to use your voice to search the web by simply saying, 'Search the web for the top performing energy stocks.'

f. Dropbox: Dropbox keeps photos, documents, videos safe and secure in one location.

g. EasyBib: EasyBib generates bibliographies by automatically citing books, journal articles, and websites just by entering the title or URLS.

h. EvernotePenultimate: EvernotePenultimate allows you to hand write notes on an iPad and to chat with other notetakers.

i. ExamVocBuilder: ExamVocBuilder uses the principle of spaced repetition with flashcards and quizzes to increase vocabulary.

j. iStudiezLite: iStudiezLite manages semesters by reminding students of assignments, exams, papers due, staying organized, managing classes, and keeping track of grades.

k. Mathway: Mathway is a #1 math problem solver that guides the student step by step through the most difficult problems. It is like having a private tutor with you all the time.

l. MyScriptSmartNote: MyScriptSmartNote enables people to handwrite their notes on a tablet. It also suggests options to complete a word or phrase. The math app allows users to create math exercises and to write complex equations.

m. Quizlet: Quizlet has millions of study stools such as flashcards, quizzes and interactive diagrams.

n. Scribd: Scribd is the largest online library with millions of documents and books. Resources related to specific courses are easy to locate.

o. ToDoList: ToDoList tracks assignments, sets reminders, bookmarks web pages and organizes planning and helping students stay productive.

2. Make a copy of the 15 apps list for each student.

The Activity

3.   Homework: Assign each student one app to present to the class. If the class is large, more than one student will be assigned the same app.

4. Each student is to prepare a 3-5 minute presentation to include: the purpose and benefits of the app, appropriate courses for the app, and a demonstration to show how to use the app.

Home Learning

After the students have learned about the 15 apps, assign one or two more apps that are relevant to their current classes and for the classes they will be taking next semester.

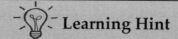
Learning Hint

Ask students to write a 300-400 word essay, "The future use of online learning."

5 | Back Pack

Studying on the Run

Course	U.S. History, U.S. Government, World History / Civilization, Economics, Geography, English Composition, Literature, Biology, Chemistry, Earth Science, Life Science, Physics, Physical Education, Health, ROTC, Discrete Math, Algebra, Geometry, Calculus, Trigonometry, Statistics, Foreign Language, Art History, Art Appreciation, Band, Music, Online Courses, Career Education
Goal	To always have study material with you
Materials needed	Class notes, handouts, textbook, Iphone, laptop, and other material that you'll textbook, pencil, paper, highlighters, flash cards and book bag
Student comments	*"I get a lot of studying done when I'm exercising, driving my car, and waiting for classes and appointments. Now I never leave my room without my study materials in my backpack."*
Professor comments	*"You can learn a lot in 5-10 minutes. 'Back Pack' helps students realize that frequent, short study sessions are so much better than trying to learn everything in an 'all-nighter'".*
Lesson duration	30-45 minutes to prepare note cards or to record information into a recorder.
Finished product to be graded	Show note cards, play information recorded on your cell phone, and any other study material in your Back Pack.

Why do I need to learn this?

It's always a good idea to have some notes and information from every course in your back pack. Put important information on note cards or in your phone. Whenever you have a few extra minutes, look at your "pocketwork".

Getting Ready for the Activity

1. Get all study materials together for each class.

The Activity

2. Put your study materials in back pack. Organize your back pack so everything will be easy to access.
3. Make sure your back pack is with you all during the day. Review the study material from your "Back Pack" whenever you have a few free minutes such as walking from place to place, exercising, or when you are waiting for someone.

Home Learning

You will become a more efficient student when you "study on the run". Try this in all your classes.

 Learning Hint

Find little blocks of time to study during the day. You'll be glad you did because you may find that by evening most of your studying is done!

6 | Beating the Nods

Course	U.S. History, U.S. Government, World History / Civilization, Economics, Geography, English Composition, Literature, Biology, Chemistry, Earth Science, Life Science, Physics, Physical Education, Health, ROTC, Discrete Math, Algebra, Geometry, Calculus, Trigonometry, Statistics, Foreign Language, Art History, Art Appreciation, Band, Music, Online Courses, Career Education
Goal	To stay awake in class
Materials needed	Mints, water, eye drops, gum
Student comments	*"I used to fall asleep during class. It was so embarrassing!! Now it's so much better---I stay awake and don't miss the information,"*
Professor comments	*"I take it personally when students fall asleep. I'm glad they are learning how to stay awake."*
Lesson duration	One class session
Finished product to be graded	Make a copy of the essay, and submit it to the college newspaper.

Why do I need to learn this?

A problem many students have is staying awake in class especially in lecture classes, boring classes, or in long classes where there is very little interaction between students and instructors. The obvious problems with falling asleep during class are that teachers don't like it and that important information will be missed.

Getting Ready for the Activity

1. Avoid taking an important class right after lunch.
2. Begin thinking of ways to stay awake during class.

The Activity

3. Ask your instructors if they have any suggestions that might help students stay awake.
4. Make a list of at least 10 ways to stay awake and alert in class and try out as many as possible. Some suggestions are: chew gum, stay hydrated (take a sip of water every ten minutes) eat mints, avoid carbohydrates at lunch because they make you sleepy, take a brisk walk before class, use eye drops, draw or doodle, drink green tea, use colored pens, ask a friend to wake you up, and keep reminding yourself how much this class costs.
5. Prepare for each class. There is less chance of falling asleep if your mind is active and if you are interested and involved in the class.
6. Write a 250-300 word essay, "How to Stay Awake in Class".

Home Learning

Before your class begins, know the techniques you will use if you become drowsy. Prepare 2-3 questions that you might ask during class.

 Learning Hint

Prepare for each class by previewing the material that will be discussed in class. Not only will this help you stay awake during class but you will find the class more interesting and you will learn more.

7 | Bold to Bold

Course	U.S. History, U.S. Government, World History / Civilization, Economics, Geography, English Composition, Literature, Biology, Chemistry, Earth Science, Life Science, Physics, Art History, Art Appreciation, Online Courses, Career Education
Goal	To improve textbook comprehension
Materials needed	A textbook with lots of major and minor headings.
Student comments	*"I have always had trouble understanding textbooks. Now that I am using 'Bold to Bold' I am actually 'thinking as I read'. My reading teacher used to warn me not to do 'mindless reading."*
Professor comments	*"'Bold to Bold' makes sense because it has students reading short sections from the textbook and then writing about what they just read. It is a great strategy for all readers—those who comprehend well and those who struggle with understanding textbook material."*
Lesson duration	Time will vary
Finished product to be graded	Show the annotated pages to your instructor.

Why do I need to learn this?

Textbook authors try to write in an organized way. One way to do this is to use a lot of headings. Reading a chapter that is separated by headings is easier to process than reading page after page of continuous text. Generally the information contained within two headings is about one concept. Bold to Bold allows the reader to grasp the meaning of information between the headings before going on to a new section. Bold to Bold is a "number one" strategy to combat mindless reading.

Getting Ready for the Activity

1. Select a chapter in your textbook which has bold headings that are used to differentiate topics.

The Activity

2. Start reading at one bold heading and read until the next bold heading.
3. Pause and think about what you just read.
4. Look over the text you just read and with a pen or pencil mark important information such as names, dates, terms and events. Use your margins to write additional information such as definitions, questions, or the main idea.
5. Continue reading using the "Bold to Bold" strategy.
6. Use all markings, questions, and marginal notes for review.

Home Learning

Students can use the "Bold to Bold" strategy for homework and then share their terms and questions with their classmates.

 Learning Hint

Writers who use a lot of bold headings in their chapters help students comprehend. The headings act as boundaries so that each concept is explained within two headings. This strategy has students read from one heading to the next and then pause and reflect about what was read before going on to the next topic.

8 | Book of Mistakes

Course	U.S. History, U.S. Government, World History / Civilization, Economics, Geography, English Composition, Literature, Biology, Chemistry, Earth Science, Life Science, Physics, Physical Education, Health, ROTC, Discrete Math, Algebra, Geometry, Calculus, Trigonometry, Statistics, Foreign Language, Art History, Art Appreciation, Band, Music, Online Courses, Career Education
Goal	To make sure you never make the same mistake again
Materials needed	Textbook, old tests, returned papers, notebook, pencil, pen, paper
Student comments	*"I barely looked at my old tests and papers and always threw them away. My "Book of Mistakes" is a record of all my errors and I'm happy to say I'll never make the same mistake!"*
Professor comments	*"Many times teachers do not instill the need to learn from mistakes. This is the surest way students will never make the same mistake again."*
Lesson duration	Time varies according to student
Finished product to be graded	Show "Book of Mistakes" notebook which contains all errors and corrections.

Why do I need to learn this?

It is always disappointing to see the errors on a returned test. It's even more disappointing when you make the same mistake a second or third time. To make sure you never make the same mistake, we recommend that you record all your mistakes (with the correct answer) in your "Book of Mistakes".

Getting Ready for the Activity

1. Get a notebook, pen, or pencil.
2. Assemble past tests and returned papers.

The Activity

3. Examine and correct very error and record them in your Book of Mistakes.
4. Review your Book of Mistakes often so you will never make the same mistake again.

Home Learning

This strategy is good for all subjects and for all mistakes. Periodically, have someone "quiz" you on your "Book of Mistakes".

 Learning Hint

Mistakes left uncorrected will leave gaps in learning, especially in classes where the content is cumulative.

9 | Cover It Up, Then Read

Course	U.S. History, U.S. Government, World History / Civilization, Economics, Geography, English Composition, Literature, Biology, Chemistry, Earth Science, Life Science, Physics, Health, Foreign Language, Art History, Art Appreciation, Online Courses, Career Education
Goal	To improve reading comprehension
Materials needed	Textbook or newspaper articles, notebook, pen, pencil
Student comments	*"I never used to read newspapers. I am surprised at all the extra things I have been learning."*
Professor comments	*"This strategy is a nice change because it has the students reading the newspaper. I try to do this strategy in my reading course at least once a week."*
Lesson duration	20-30 minutes
Finished product to be graded	Show the running record of all the articles you have read to your instructor. You may want to offer a demonstration of this strategy in another class.

Why do I need to learn this?

Students with weak comprehension skills have a serious disadvantage because most college textbooks are written at advanced levels. "Cover It Up, Then Read" guides the student to determine the main idea (the most important reading skill). (A Pre-med student used this strategy to prepare for the verbal portion of the MCAT. She said it helped her a lot and her highest score on the admissions test for medical school was in reading).

Getting Ready for the Activity

1.   Choose 3-4 pages from a chapter in a textbook or newspaper with headings.

The Activity

2.   Cover up the heading. Begin by reading the first two paragraphs. Stop reading and ask yourself, "What is the topic?" Then ask, "What is said about the topic?" The answer to this will give the main idea.

3.   Uncover the heading and check to see if your main idea is similar to the heading.

4.   Complete reading any remaining paragraphs. The rest of the information will be the details and facts that support the main idea.

5.   Write the name and date of the newspaper in your notebook

6.   Keep a running record of all the articles you have read.

Home Learning

It usually takes a lot of time and practice to improve reading comprehension. This strategy should be practiced frequently outside of class.

 Learning Hint

Understanding the main idea is the first and most important step in the reading comprehension process. All the details and facts explain and develop the main idea. "Cover It Up, Then Read" requires the reader to be actively involved with reading.

10 | Crossword Puzzle Maker

Course	U.S. History, U.S. Government, World History / Civilization, Economics, Geography, English Composition, Literature, Biology, Chemistry, Earth Science, Life Science, Physics, Health, Foreign Language, Art History, Art Appreciation, Online Courses, Career Education
Goal	To learn vocabulary and terms for upcoming tests.
Materials needed	Internet, printer, and material that needs to be learned for a test
Student comments	*"Doing this strategy is a lot of fun. It sure is an easy way to learn vocabulary!"*
Professor comments	*"Although this strategy takes a lot of time, it's worthwhile because the students think it's like playing a game."*
Lesson duration	50 – 60 minutes
Finished product to be graded	Make a copy of the completed crossword puzzle with correct answers.

Why do I need to learn this?

"Crossword Puzzle Maker" is an enjoyable way to learn vocabulary, terms, and facts for an upcoming test. You will be creating your own crossword puzzle.

Getting Ready for the Activity

1. Make a list of approximately 15 – 30 vocabulary words, terms, and facts with the definitions that you need to know.

The Activity

2. Choose a free online crossword puzzle maker.
3. Create your own crossword puzzle according to the online puzzle directions. You will need to write a definition for each term.
4. After you have followed the directions from the puzzle maker site, print out several copies and test yourself. Review often until all the words are known.

Home Learning

You may want to try some other puzzles and word games on puzzle sites.

 Learning Hint

Use puzzle maker resources for all content areas. Use puzzle maker with a study partner.

11 | Dictionary, Check It

Course	U.S. History, U.S. Government, World History / Civilization, Economics, Geography, English Composition, Literature, Biology, Chemistry, Earth Science, Life Science, Physics, Physical Education, Health, Discrete Math, Algebra, Geometry, Calculus, Trigonometry, Statistics, Foreign Language, Art History, Art Appreciation, Online Courses, Career Education
Goal	To learn word meanings
Materials needed	Pocket dictionary
Student comments	*"Now I always carry my pocket dictionary around. It's so easy to learn the new words. My vocabulary has grown!"*
Professor comments	*"This strategy is a 'must' for students trying to build a college vocabulary. It's so effortless---I like it because it's so easy to review the words."*
Lesson duration	Varies according to the number of words needed to learn
Finished product to be graded	Show your instructor your dictionary. Ask your instructor to give you a quiz on all the words that you have checked.

Why do I need to learn this?

Have you ever looked up an unknown word in the dictionary and then forgotten its meaning after a day or two? This is a common problem and to make matters worse—since you forgot the word, you needed to look it up again and again!! The "Dictionary, Check it" is an effortless strategy that is bound to help you increase your vocabulary.

Getting Ready for the Activity

1. Get your materials together: a paperback dictionary, pencil, and textbook

The Activity

2. When encountering an unfamiliar word, look it up in the pocket dictionary. Then underline the meaning and put a check mark next to the word.

3. In all likelihood you will have to look up the word another time (it takes many encounters to learn a word). When you have to look up the word again put another check next to it. Don't be surprised if it takes 3 times (3 checks) to learn the word.

4. Thumb through your pocket dictionary during your spare time to reinforce learning the new words.

Home Learning

Keep your pocket dictionary in your back pack and every time you have a few moments, take it out and quiz yourself on the checked words.

 Learning Hint

To make sure you know the words you have "checked", use them in writing and in speaking.

31

12 | Five Minute Summary With Laptop

Course	U.S. History, U.S. Government, World History / Civilization, Economics, Geography, English Composition, Literature, Biology, Chemistry, Earth Science, Life Science, Physics, Health, Foreign Language, Art History, Art Appreciation, Career Education
Goal	To retain a high level of information recently learned by providing a review session during the last five minutes of class.
Materials needed	Class notes, laptop
Student comments	*"The five minutes I spend right after class has made such a difference in my grade. I save a lot of time by reviewing the material right away."*
Professor comments	*"I encourage all my students to take five minutes after class time so everyone can do the "Five Minute Summary with Technology". Sometimes I leave five minutes at the end of class so everyone can write a summary."*
Lesson duration	5-10 minutes
Finished product to be graded	Make copies of your Five Minute Summaries.

Why do I need to learn this?

Students are expected to remember a lot of information that is presented in class. Although students are reminded to review within 24 hours, most students wait and review a day or two before an exam. This strategy helps combat the high rate of forgetting because the review takes place immediately.

The "Five Minute Summary with Technology" gives students the opportunity to "revisit" the new information. Students use the five minutes to write as much as they can remember without referring to their notes.

Getting Ready for the Activity

1. Become an active listener during the entire class period.

The Activity

2. Take notes on your laptop.
3. Set aside five minutes after class and go to a new page on your laptop and write as much information as you can remember without looking at your notes.
4. At the end of five minutes, stop writing and read what you just wrote.
5. Note any concepts, information and terminology that need clarification.
6. That evening clarify information so your Five Minute Summary is complete.
7. Keep your summaries with your other study materials for exam preparation.

Home Learning

Compare your summary with your actual class notes. Use all materials to predict future test questions.

 Learning Hint

Consult language arts textbooks or internet for writing summary guidelines and sample summaries.

13 | Friend to Friend

Course	U.S. History, U.S. Government, World History / Civilization, Economics, Geography, English Composition, Literature, Biology, Chemistry, Earth Science, Life Science, Physics, Health, ROTC, Discrete Math, Algebra, Geometry, Calculus, Trigonometry, Statistics, Foreign Language, Art History, Art Appreciation, Career Education
Goal	To increase the amount of information presented in class
Materials needed	Internet, folder
Student comments	*"Another student and I started emailing and then we added another student---so every night I get 2 emails about the most important information.""*
Professor comments	*"Friend to Friend is a good example of collaborative learning."*
Lesson duration	15-20 minutes
Finished product to be graded	Make copies of all emails you sent and copies of the emails you received.

Why do I need to learn this?

There will be many times in every class when you are not able to capture and remember all the information. "Friend to Friend" is the strategy that boosts learning by sharing information with a classmate. Both of you will benefit because each of you are sharing your perception of "the most important information."

Getting Ready for the Activity

1. Find a dependable "classmate" in the class who agrees to participate in this strategy. Exchange email addresses.

The Activity

2. After the class, edit your notes and identify 4 to 5 concepts that you consider to be the most important ones.
3. Send an email to your "friend" and write the 4-5 important concepts along with 2-3 questions that you think your professor might ask about the concepts. Send the email.
4. Your "friend" will also send you an email with the 4-5 concepts he or she believed to be the most important along with 2-3 questions that the professor might ask.
5. Make a copy of both emails, read them, put them in a folder, and review often before each exam.

Home Learning

The significant advantage of "Friend to Friend" is that you are getting another person's point of view on what they consider to be the most concepts. You may need to consult the textbook to verify and answer the questions sent in the emails.

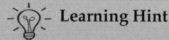 **Learning Hint**

Exchanging highlights from each class with a friend is a worthwhile activity. It promotes collaboration and keeping up with each class.

14 | How to Deal with Professors

Course	U.S. History, U.S. Government, World History / Civilization, Economics, Geography, English Composition, Literature, Biology, Chemistry, Earth Science, Life Science, Physics, Health, Discrete Math, Algebra, Geometry, Calculus, Trigonometry, Statistics, Foreign Language, Art History, Art Appreciation, Band, Music, Career Education
Goal	To establish good relationships with your professors
Materials needed	-----
Student comments	*"I am so glad I got to know my professor. I visited him during office hours. We talked a lot about lots of things. I know he will give me a good recommendation."*
Professor comments	*"All professors appreciate students who are friendly, interested, and polite. It's a shame some students lack basic social skills."*
Lesson duration	Varies
Finished product to be graded	Make a list of "How to Deal with Professors". Show it to your instructor and submit it to the college newspaper.

Why do I need to learn this?

Although most professors are friendly and helpful, you may find some are aloof. It is in your best interest to get to know all of your professors because there are many benefits to establishing a positive student / professor relationship.

Getting Ready for the Activity

1. Before you attend your first class, think about the way you want your professor to perceive you. Put yourself in your professor's position. Wouldn't you like your students to walk in with a smile and say hello?

The Activity

2. Some basic ways to establish a relationship with your instructor are to greet him or her, make occasional eye contact, attend class regularly, be on time, refrain from side conversations during class, avoid putting your head down on the desk, or sleep, be interested in the class, avoid asking for special favors, don't eat during class, and, in general, maintain suitable class behavior.

3. Turn in assignments on time, take responsibility in case you receive a poor grade, and if you disagree do it tactfully and respectfully.

4. Visit your professor at least once during office hours.

5. Once in a while stop by after class for a quick conversation.

6. Follow the "rules and regulations" of the class which are usually stated in the syllabus. Don't ask the professor to "break the rules" for you.

7. Ask your professor if he or she has any "pet peeves" or preferences in the way students conduct themselves.

8. When the course is over for the semester, make sure you greet your professor if you should meet again. You never know when you may need a favor (like a letter of recommendation).

9. Think about the other ways you might establish a good relationship with the professors you have this semester. Write them down and make an effort to do most of them.

Home Learning

Ask some of your friends and classmates about some of the things they do to get along with their professor. Interview several professors and ask them their expectations of student behavior. Write a summary and report your findings in the school newspaper.

> ### Learning Hint
>
> Your success in college is not entirely dependent on grades. The impression you give your professor can have a positive or negative effect on your overall performance in the class. Teachers, for the most part, like their profession and they especially like respectful, well-mannered students.

15 | Legal Cheat Sheet

Course	U.S. History, U.S. Government, World History/Civilization, Economics, Geography, English Composition, Literature, Biology, Chemistry, Earth Science, Life Science, Physics, Health, Discrete Math, Algebra, Geometry, Calculus, Trigonometry, Statistics, Foreign Language, Art History, Art Appreciation, Career Education
Goal	To receive an A on an upcoming test
Materials needed	All materials that need to be studied for the test, pencil or pen, paper
Student comments	*"I like making 'Legal Cheat Sheets'. I read them over and over and made an A on the test"*
Professor comments	*"I think all students should make their own legal cheat sheets. This is so much better than having teachers make study guides."*
Lesson duration	1-2 hours
Finished product to be graded	Turn in a copy of your "Legal Cheat Sheet".

Why do I need to learn this?

A test only samples some of the material that might be on a test. Even though a professor might say the test is on four chapters, class notes, and handouts, not all the material will be asked on the test. Those students who make good grades generally have a good idea of what will be on the test. They select what they consider to be the essential information and write it on one sheet of paper (front and back). This becomes their "legal cheat sheet" and can be used to review right up until test time!!

Getting Ready for the Strategy

1. At least four days before the test assemble all material that needs to be reviewed.

The Activity

summary phrases for text

2. With a pen or pencil mark only the information that you think will be on the test.
3. Since you will only be using the front and back of one sheet of paper, be very selective—choose information that you definitely need to study. Don't waste space writing something you already know.
4. Fill both sides of your "Legal Cheat Sheet."
5. Review your "Legal Cheat Sheet" right up until the test.

Home Learning

Have a friend also make a "Legal Cheat Sheet" and share with each other.

> ### Learning Hint
> The more you know about a subject, the more likely you will be able to predict test questions.

16 | Lock Screen

Course	U.S. History, U.S. Government, World History / Civilization, Economics, Geography, English Composition, Literature, Biology, Chemistry, Earth Science, Life Science, Physics, Health, Discrete Math, Algebra, Geometry, Calculus, Trigonometry, Statistics, Foreign Language, Art History, Art Appreciation, Online Courses, Career Education
Goal	To memorize information
Materials needed	Cell phone and all material that needs to be memorized
Student comments	*"I love using 'Lock Screen' because I don't even realize I'm memorizing. It makes memorizing so easy!"*
Instructor comments	*"'After a student told me about 'Lock Screen' I gave the class an assignment—I asked them to take photos of 3 geometry formulas and use them on 'Lock Screen'. One week later I gave them a geometry quiz based on the formulas and most of the students got everything correct because they all knew the formulas --a great strategy."*
Lesson Duration	Time will vary
Finished product to be graded	Show instructor 3 photos used on 'Lock Screen'.

Why do I need to learn this?

Every course usually has material that must be committed to memory. Math formulas, diagrams, process charts, the chemical periodic table, and vocabulary definitions are just a few examples that students will be expected to know. Every time the student uses the phone, the first thing he/she will see is the photo of the material to be memorized. Since the average teenager uses the phone at least fifty times a day, he/she will see the photo fifty times and it will, in most cases, be memorized with a minimum amount of effort!

Getting Ready for the Activity

1. Explain to the class how 'Lock Screen' will be used to memorize information.
2. Remind students to bring their cell phones and textbook to the next class.
3. Select several diagrams, vocabulary words, formulas or other material that should be memorized. In an anatomy class, an illustration of the bones, nerves, and circulatory system are examples that should be memorized.

The Activity

4. Instruct students to photograph the material that was selected (#3)
5. Go to 'camera roll' and set one photo on the 'wallpaper' screen.
6. Every time the student uses the phone, the photo will be seen and before long it will be memorized.
7. Select new photo to be on the "Lock Screen". Repeat until 3 photos have been on "Lock Screen".
8. Give a "mock test" on the materials selected to be put on "Lock Screen".

42

Home Learning

When reviewing, ask a family member to give you a quiz on the photos you used with "Lock Screen".

Learning Hint

Use the learning strategy "Teach It" to explain (out loud) each photo used in "Lock Screen".

17 | Make A Test

Course	U.S. History, U.S. Government, World History / Civilization, Economics, Geography, English Composition, Literature, Biology, Chemistry, Earth Science, Life Science, Physics, Health, Discrete Math, Algebra, Geometry, Calculus, Trigonometry, Statistics, Foreign Language, Art History, Art Appreciation, Online Courses, Career Education
Goal	To get a high grade on a test
Materials needed	Study materials for the test, pencil, pen, paper
Student comments	*"This is my favorite strategy. When I studied for my last test I made 90 questions and answers. There were about 50 questions on the test and I predicted about 30 of them."*
Professor comments	*"I encourage my students to make a mock test. Sometimes I have my students prepare 15 questions and answers or homework. Then during class review they take turns giving the 'mock test' to their classmates.*
Lesson duration	50 – 60 minutes
Finished product to be graded	Turn in a copy of your 'mock test'.

Why do I need to learn this?

"Make A Test" is an active way to study for a test. Most students just look over their notes and/or reread the textbook---these are passive activities.

Getting Ready for the Activity

1.   Gather all materials that need to be studied for an upcoming test.

The Activity

2.   Write at least twice the amount of questions that will be on the test. Use one side of the paper for the question and the other side for the answer.

3.   Use your "test" by answering each question. Give yourself time to recall the answer from memory. Check the other side for the correct answer.

Home Learning

Ask a family member or friend to ask you all questions. Ask them to "mix up" the order of questions.

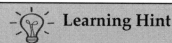 **Learning Hint**

It is always a good idea to study with questions when preparing for tests. Use both factual and inferential type questions.

18 | My To-Do List

Course	U.S. History, U.S. Government, World History / Civilization, Economics, Geography, English Composition, Literature, Biology, Chemistry, Earth Science, Life Science, Physics, Physical Education, Health, ROTC, Discrete Math, Algebra, Geometry, Calculus, Trigonometry, Statistics, Foreign Language, Art History, Art Appreciation, Band, Music, Online Courses, Career Education
Goal	To make sure all assignments and obligations are completed
Materials needed	Syllabus for each class, calendar, small notebook, pencil, pen, paper
Student comments	*"Now I never forget anything. I used to be so unorganized but now I like getting everything done on time. In fact, since I started making To-Do lists, I have more free time."*
Professor comments:	*"It's usually my very good students who make To-Do lists. They save time and stay organized. Everyone, not only students, should get into the habit of making a To-Do list."*
Lesson duration	40 – 60 minutes
Finished product to be graded	Make a copy of all "To-Do-Lists" and show them to your instructor along with your planner.

Why do I need to learn this?

College students have many responsibilities. Forgetting to do some of them could have serious consequences such as not showing up at a meeting with a professor, forgetting to take a final exam, or not paying a bill.

Getting Ready for the Activity

1. Assemble a calendar, syllabus for each class, small notebook, pen or pencil.

The Activity

2. Decide whether your To-Do List will be Daily or Weekly.
3. For Weekly To-Do Lists: On Sunday night consult your calendar and syllabi for all important due dates, test dates, assignments, meetings, practices, social events, birthdays, anniversaries, bills to be paid, and anything else that needs to be accomplished that week. Write all items that need to be accomplished that week in the small notebook.

classes

4. For Daily To-Do Lists: On the night before or in the morning consult your calendar and syllabi and write in your small notebook all the things you hope to accomplish that day.
5. Keep the small notebook with the To-Do Lists with you so you can "check off" completed items.

Home Learning
The 5-10 minutes it takes to make a "To-Do List" can save you hours later on!

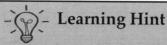 **Learning Hint**

It is a good feeling when you have accomplished everything on your "To-Do List"

19 | Once Upon A Time

Course	U.S. History, U.S. Government, World History / Civilization, Economics, Geography, Literature, Biology, Chemistry, Earth Science, Life Science, Physics, Health, Art History, Art Appreciation, Online Courses, Career Education
Goal	To remember information in a story (narrative) format
Materials needed	Textbook, pencil, pen, paper
Student comments	*"It's so easy to remember a story. I like using my imagination and all my classmates want to hear my stories!"*
Professor comments	*"We tried this strategy in a biology class. It was a lesson about how phagocytes destroy germs. The students were so imaginative and the stories were great."*
Lesson duration	50-60 minutes
Finished product to be graded	Make a copy of your "Once Upon A Time" story.

Why do I need to learn this?

It is usually easier to remember a story than trying to remember textbook information. This strategy can turn a dull subject into an interesting and entertaining story.

Getting Ready for the Activity

1.   Choose a textbook reading assignment.

The Activity

2.   Read the selection.
3.   Turn the selection into a story by saying, "Once upon a time, there-----"
4.   An example of this strategy is given below. Several pages in a geography textbook described "The Black Triangle". Read the paragraph below to see how an expository section was turned into a story.

"Once upon a time the forests in Germany, Poland, and the Czech Republic were beautiful and free of pollution. People loved the beauty of their forests with lakes, rivers, trees, and animals. Every Sunday you would find hundreds of families picnicking in the countryside. Then a terrible thing happened. The Communists took over and built mines, coal powered plants, factories that produced toxic pollutants and poisons that destroyed the atmosphere, rivers, lakes, and land. The forests became industrialized. The most severe area destroyed was called The Black Triangle which included the Sudety Mountains of the Czech Republic. Acid rain and heavy metals such as mercury, lead, coal mine salts, and organic carcinogens can still be found in the region today but, thanks to United Nations Economic Commission for Europe, there have been massive efforts to restore the land. Today, people living there have more health problems and lower life expectancy as a result of the pollutants. Although it will take many; more years and great expense to restore The Black Triangle, some people recently have said that they see signs of a new triangle—"The Green Triangle".

5.   Read the story you created from your textbook reading assignment several times before the test.

Home Learning

After you have written a few "stories" from your expository textbook, read them to a friend or family member. On the next day ask them to repeat the story. You will find that they probably remembered most of the story.

Learning Hint

If you have a creative mind or a lively imagination, you will enjoy this strategy.

20 | Pace Reading

Course	U.S. History, U.S. Government, World History / Civilization, Economics, Geography, English Composition, Literature, Biology, Chemistry, Earth Science, Life Science, Physics, Health, Art History, Art Appreciation, Online Courses, Career Education
Goal	To improve reading comprehension by marking important sentences in the text.
Materials needed	Textbook, pencil, and highlighter
Student comments	*"I like checking the important sentences. It's fun and not boring. I got a good grade on the test!"*
Professor comments	*"I like the strategy; because it has the student reading the same material 2-3 times. I try to impress upon them that dense material should be read several times."*
Lesson duration	40 – 60 minutes
Finished product to be graded	Show the section of the textbook with checked sentences.

Why do I need to learn this?

Many students underline important information in their text as a memory and learning tool. Often students underline practically everything! The problem is that most students have difficulty separating the "wheat from the chaff". This strategy offers a solution. It will help students make a better choice on what and how much to underline or highlight. It also helps students read more in less time.

Getting Ready for the Activity

1. Choose a content textbook from one of your classes.
2. Go to the next assigned chapter.
   If there is a chapter that needs rereading, then use that chapter.
   The course syllabus can be consulted in making a decision on what chapter to use.

The Activity

3. Begin reading the chapter with a pencil.
4. Use the pencil to check each sentence that is important and should be kept.
   Place a check next to the sentence in the right margin.
5. Read to the end of the paragraph or section.
6. Reread all the checked sentences.
7. Highlight those checked sentences that are important and should be kept.
   Some of your previously checked sentences may no longer be very important. Do not highlight these.
8. The highlighted sentences should be reviewed periodically before the exam.

Home Learning

Continue using Pace Reading until the chapter is finished. Then go back and study the highlighted information and review the checked information.

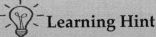**Learning Hint**
Pace Reading helps students stay focused on the reading task. It also helps them to be selective about what they highlight.

21 | Powerful Power Points

Course	U.S. History, U.S. Government, World History / Civilization, Economics, Geography, English Composition, Literature, Biology, Chemistry, Earth Science, Life Science, Physics, Health, ROTC, Discrete Math, Algebra, Geometry, Calculus, Trigonometry, Statistics, Art History, Art Appreciation, Career Education
Goal	To increase amount of learning in lecture classes.
Materials needed	2 copies of power point presentations, pencil, pen,
Student comments	*"In lecture classes I write a lot of information. But when class is over I try to make sense of what I should have learned. I use the first set to group and organize the information and then I copy it neatly on the other set."*
Professor comments	*"In lecture classes I expect my students to add more information to the power point slides. This strategy has them go one step further. It has them organize the information so everything is put together in a meaningful way."*
Lesson duration	40 – 60 minutes.
Finished product to be graded	Show your instructor both copies of power point presentations.

Why do I need to learn this?

There is definitely an advantage to take lecture notes on power point handouts because each slide gives you a "snapshot" of the lecture. Remember, that a power point slide only gives you a limited amount of information----this is why you must add more information.

Getting Ready for the Activity

1. Print out two sets of power point handouts before class.

The Activity

2. Take a lot of notes on the first set of power point handouts.
3. Within 24 hours open your textbook to the same information that was presented in class. Begin editing your first set of power point notes and add additional information from the text that you think is important.
4. After you have edited and reviewed the first set of power point handouts, transfer that information to the second set of power points. Organize the information so you are able to "see" the main points and related details.
5. The second set of power point handouts should be used to review. You can use colored markers to highlight concepts and terms as well as making up text questions you think might be on the test.

Home Learning

Use your second set of Power Points and recite the information in your own words. Recreate the lecture using your lecture notes.

> **Learning Hint**
>
> Although every slide in a power point is important, it is only part of the brief version or an outline. The complete version is given in the total oral presentation of the lecture or in the textbook. This means that it is your responsibility to add information to the power point slides until you have the thorough, complete version.

22 | Rap

Course	U.S. History, U.S. Government, World History / Civilization, Economics, Geography, Literature, Biology, Chemistry, Earth Science, Life Science, Physics, Health, Discrete Math, Algebra, Geometry, Calculus, Trigonometry, Statistics, Foreign Language, Art History, Art Appreciation, Band, Music, Online Courses, Career Education
Goal	To help remember concepts, main ideas, supporting details, and vocabulary by creating a poem or rap.
Materials needed	All materials that need to be reviewed for a test
Student comments	*"At first I didn't want to do this but now I usually do one poem for every major test. This strategy is a lot of fun."*
Professor comments	*"In a last review session several students read their 'Rap'--they were very clever and all the students said they learned a lot from hearing them."*
Lesson duration	Amount of time will vary
Finished product to be graded	Submit "Rap" or poem

Why do I need to learn this?

College tests usually cover a lot of information that must be remembered. "Rap" is a motivating strategy that makes remembering easy because students use the material to create a "catchy" poem or rap.

Getting Ready for the Activity

1.   Before the next test, select material that needs to be learned. Include class notes, handouts, and textbook chapters.

The Activity

2.   Begin your poem or rap by selecting the main idea (The title is often the main idea).
3.   Add supporting details and important terms and vocabulary.
4.   Add "powerful", vibrant adjectives and verbs to make your poem or rap memorable.
5.   Try to make your poem or rap "rhyme and click".
6.   Edit your poem or rap and make sure it includes all the main ideas, supporting details, and vocabulary you need to learn for the test.
7.   Write your final draft.
8.   Recite your poem many times before the test.

Home Learning

Write another poem from a different section or chapter. Consult a rhyming dictionary for added impact!

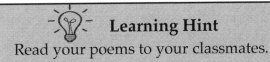

Learning Hint
Read your poems to your classmates.

23 | Say It, Then Play It

Course	U.S. History, U.S. Government, World History/Civilization, Economics, Geography, English Composition, Literature, Biology, Chemistry, Earth Science, Life Science, Physics, Health, Discrete Math, Algebra, Geometry, Calculus, Trigonometry, Statistics, Foreign Language, Art History, Art Appreciation, Band, Music, Online Courses, Career Education
Goal	To increase understanding by listening
Materials needed	Textbook, class notes, smartphone
Student comments	*"Now I record all my notes and I've just started recording important parts of my textbook. It's really helpful because I learn well by listening."*
Professor comments	*"This strategy is really helpful for auditory learners. If they have a recording of all their class notes, they should do very well in my course."*
Lesson duration	30 – 60 minutes
Finished product to be graded	Either send your instructor the recordings or show your instructor how you used your smart phone to record textbook information.

Why do I need to learn this?

Do your eyes become tired after a two hour study session? Do you ever get bored reading chapter after chapter? "Say It, Then Play It" is a strategy that you can do while driving, exercising, or lying in bed. It is especially good for auditory learners and for everyone who needs a little variety in studying.

Getting Ready for the Activity

1. Select material (class notes and textbook pages) that need reviewing for a test.
2. Obtain an audio recorder or smartphone in good working condition.

The Activity

3. Begin reading your class notes into the recorder.
4. Find corresponding information from the textbook and read that information into the recorder.
5. Listen to recordings.

Home Learning

Preview the next chapter by reading at least 3-4 pages into the recorder. Listen to the recording before that material is explained in class.

Learning Hint

Often reading and rereading are the only strategies students use. Although it's true that most students are visual learners, every student will benefit when an additional modality, such as listening, is also used. The technology available today makes "Say It, Then Play It" easy to use. Another feature of the strategy is that both sides of the brain are being used.

---

24 | Sketch Book Journal

Course	U.S. History, U.S. Government, World History / Civilization, Economics, Geography, English Composition, Literature, Biology, Chemistry, Earth Science, Life Science, Physics, Health, ROTC, Discrete Math, Algebra, Geometry, Calculus, Trigonometry, Statistics, Art History, Art Appreciation, Online Courses, Career Education
Goal	To improve comprehension by visual means
Materials needed	Textbook, journal, pencil, pen, paper, colored markers
Student comments	*"I started making a sketch book journal for biology and since then I am getting higher grades. I like the strategy and I like it that all the 'sketches' are together in one journal."*
Professor comments	*"This is an excellent strategy because it's true that making your own drawing helps learning more than just looking at a drawing in a book."*
Lesson duration	20 – 40 minutes per sketch
Finished product to be graded	Show your instructor your "Sketch Book Journal".

Why do I need to learn this?

It is easier to remember a picture than the printed word. And it is even easier to remember a picture that you drew yourself.

Getting Ready for the Activity

1. You will probably want to do this exercise with a text from the biological sciences, chemistry, or physics. Choose one.

The Activity

2. Sketch visuals from the text, concepts learned, processes discussed (i.e. mitosis) and anything that reinforces understanding.
3. Label each sketch with name of topic, date, chapter and page number. Make sure your sketches are colorful
4. Write a brief description of your sketch. Explain it in your own words.
5. Label parts and section of your sketch.

Home Learning

Study your sketch while reading your notes for an exam.

> ### Learning Hint
> Be sure to note the details that are found in the book or internet that should be in your sketch. Your sketches do not have to be perfectly drawn—they should be functional and understandable to you. Make sure they are in color. This will help you recall information for the test.

25 │ SQ3R Modified for College

Course	U.S. History, U.S. Government, World History / Civilization, Economics, Geography, English Composition, Literature, Biology, Chemistry, Earth Science, Life Science, Physics, Health, Art History, Art Appreciation, Online Courses, Career Education
Goal	To learn textual information
Materials needed	Textbook, pencil, pen, paper
Student comments	*"It's a lot of work and takes a lot of time but I really learned a lot and got an A on my test."*
Professor comments	*"SQ3R is a 'tried and true' learning strategy. I especially like the 'recite' stage."*
Lesson duration	45 – 60 minutes
Finished product to be graded	Show your instructor the headings that you turned into questions and how you highlighted in the text to answer the questions.

Why do I need to learn this?

SQ3R Modified for College helps you make a mock test from the assigned reading. It is a study "short-cut" and saves time because the material is written in the text and you only have to mark it for study. The beauty of this strategy is that it helps you select and mark the most important information you need to know in the text so you do not end up highlighting the entire paragraph or section.

Getting Ready for the Activity

1. **Survey**: Begin by building knowledge about the chapter before you begin to read. You can build knowledge by following these steps below:

   a. Read the title and introductory paragraph(s). Grasp the name of the chapter. Usually the introduction gives the background of the topic, the summary of what is to be learned and the purpose for learning the information.

   b. After reading the introduction, read the subheadings and italicized words. This means to read through the chapter heading by heading. Do not bother to read the material within the headings at this time. Just reading the headings will give you a conceptualized outline of information in the chapter.

   c. Finally, read the summary at the end of the chapter. The summary is a restatement of what was presented in the entire chapter. If your chapter does not have a summary, read the last paragraph at the end of each heading section.

The Activity

2. **Question**: Using a pen or pencil, turn the first heading into a question. Use when, why, where, what, an how to formulate your question. You should be able to write a good strong question because of the prior knowledge you built in the survey section. Keep in mind the type of quiz or test questions your professor is likely to ask.

3. **Read**: Now read for the answer to the question. Highlight the answer to the question. If you feel the need to highlight other information, highlight it in a different color.

4. **Recite**: Before reading the next section, close the book and see if you can recite to yourself all the information in the section you just read. Make sure you can recite the answer to your question. Remember, this will probably be a test question.

5. Continue reading each section using steps 2-3 (question and recite).

6. **Review**: Go through all of the heading questions and see if you can answer all of the questions without the aid of the book. Make sure you can fully answer the questions by telling yourself the concepts, main points, and sub points.

Home Learning

Make a mock test. Practice taking the test in the time frame that you will have in class. Check your answers in the text.

Learning Hint

Listed below are question word prompts to help you formulate your questions.

Define	Describe	Label	List	Name
Outline	Reproduce	Select	State	Convert
Distinguish	Estimate	Explain	Generate	Paraphrase
Calculate	Examine	Classify	Relate	Interpret
Differentiate	Breakdown	Infer	Rank	Solve
Predict	Create	Compose	Design	Develop
Assess	Critique	Evaluate	Judge	Justify

---

26 | Summertime Smarts

Course	U.S. History, U.S. Government, World History / Civilization, Economics, Geography, English Composition, Literature, Biology, Chemistry, Earth Science, Life Science, Physics, Physical Education, Health, ROTC, Discrete Math, Algebra, Geometry, Calculus, Trigonometry, Statistics, Foreign Language, Art History, Art Appreciation, Band, Music, Online Courses, Career Education
Goal	To get a "head start" before classes begin
Materials needed	syllabi and textbooks for future classes to be taken next semester, journal, internet, textbook, pencil, pen, paper
Student comments	*"Summertime Smarts gave me a 'heads-up' when classes began because I already knew a lot. I made A's on the first quizzes and tests I took."*
Professor comments	*"Students who have some background knowledge about a course naturally have an advantage. It's more difficult to learn something new if there is no prior knowledge.*
Lesson duration	Varies with each student
Finished product to be graded	Show your journal to your instructor

Why do I need to learn this?

The more you know about a topic, the easier it is to learn new information about that topic. If you are taking a challenging course next semester, use some free time between semesters to get a "head start" by learning some of the basic information that will be given in class. It is a great confidence booster to be in a class and already know a lot of the information. A little preparation can make a huge difference!

Getting Ready for the Activity

1.   Get a syllabus for the next class you will be taking so you will know the requirements and materials needed for the class.

The Activity

2.   Buy the textbook and other materials required for the class.
3.   Go to the library and get several books on the same topic.
4.   Search the internet for videos and information about the topics that will covered in class.
5.   Begin reading at least one hour a day. Watch the videos. Learn the specific vocabulary and terms. Use your other resources. For example, if you are learning about the Korean or the Vietnam War, you may want to interview a few former soldiers from these wars.
6.   Keep a journal of all the activities for "Summertime Smarts". Explain how and why each resource contributed to the background knowledge you needed.

Home Learning

This is an opportunity to learn at your own pace without worrying about tests. This is actually learning for the sake of learning. The benefit will be when you begin taking the class and realize that you already know so much.

> ### 💡 Learning Hint
>
> "Summertime Smarts" makes learning fun. It will help reduce stress and it should help you earn a good grade in the class. Remember, that the most important factor in reading comprehension is background knowledge. "Summertime Smarts" is a great way to help you become the student you want to be!

27 | Twenty Most Important Things

Course	U.S. History, U.S. Government, World History / Civilization, Economics, Geography, English Composition, Literature, Biology, Chemistry, Earth Science, Life Science, Physics, Health, ROTC, Discrete Math, Algebra, Geometry, Calculus, Trigonometry, Statistics, Foreign Language, Art History, Art Appreciation, Online Courses, Career Education
Goal	To reduce the amount of study material to the twenty most important things that might be on a test
Materials needed	All materials that you need to study for a test, a few 4x6 index cards, paper, pencil or pen
Student comments	*"It's hard to only choose 20 important things when studying for a test because everything seems important. It took me a lot of time to get my list down to 20 but as I was doing this, I realized I was learning a lot."*
Teacher comments	*"Some information is obviously going to be more important that others and some material more than other material will more likely be on a test."*
Lesson Duration	50-60 minutes
Individual or group	Begins as an individual project and then shared with the group
Finished product to be graded	Submit a copy of your "Twenty Most Important Things".

Why do I need to learn this?

As students spend time trying to select "The Twenty Most Important Things", they are learning the material. In a way, this is what many teachers do when making tests.

Getting Ready for the Activity

1.   Two to three days before a test, gather the notes, handouts, and textbook.

The Activity

2.   Read through and put a mark next to a term, concept, name, date and anything else that is important and that might be on a test.
3.   Refer to everything that is marked and try to reduce all the marked items until there are only twenty of the most important things.
4.   Review these twenty items. Share your list with a classmate's list.

Home Learning

When studying for a comprehensive test that has 4-5 chapters, you may want to use "The Twenty Most Important Things" in each chapter.

 Learning Hint

If students have difficulty generating their own questions for "The Twenty Most Important Things", encourage them to use these question prompts: *discuss, explain, examine, paraphrase,* and *develop.*

28 | The Take-Apart Notebook

Course	U.S. History, U.S. Government, World History / Civilization, Economics, Geography, English Composition, Literature, Biology, Chemistry, Earth Science, Life Science, Physics, Health, Discrete Math, Algebra, Geometry, Calculus, Trigonometry, Statistics, Foreign Language, Art History, Art Appreciation, Online Courses, Career Education
Goal	To coordinate textbook and classroom information
Materials needed	Textbook that has been put in a binder, pencil, pen, and paper
Student comments	*"It's great not having to carry around heavy textbooks. Now I can read and glance through the textbook while listening to the instructor."*
Professor comments	*"I also put the textbook in a binder and take to class the section I will be lecturing about that day. It's great for students to write their class notes right in the book---this makes sense."*
Lesson Duration:	1 hour to have the textbook put in a binder
Finished product to be graded	Bring your "Take-Apart Notebook" containing the textbook which has been put in a binder.

Why do I need to learn this?

Taking your textbooks to class everyday can be a burden, yet many people say that it's a good idea to read along while your instructor lectures from the book. The "Take-Apart Notebook" is a strategy that allows you to have your text next to you as you listen and take notes. When you do this, your understanding will improve because you have the instructor's lecture along with the related textbook information. You are combining the information! Don't forget that most instructors give tests on both class and textbook information.

Getting Ready for the Activity

1. During the early part of the semester, bring your textbook to a copy center.
2. Remove the binding and cover.
3. Punch 3 holes in all the pages of the book.
4. Place all pages of the book in a 3-ring binder.

The Activity

5. Read the syllabus to determine the pages in the text that will be discussed in class and remove these pages from the 3-ring binder.
6. As you take notes in class, refer to textbook pages so lecture and text information is combined.
7. Punch holes in class notes and in handouts and place in 3-ring binder so all information is in one place.

Home Learning

Within 24 hours after class, read your class notes and the pages from the textbook you brought with you to class. Combine your class notes with the textbook pages. You may want to make a Take-Apart Notebook for all your courses.

Learning Hint

Unfortunately, many students never read their textbook. They just learn the information presented in class. Other students may wait until the night before an exam to read their textbook. The "Take-Apart Notebook" has students learning lecture and text information at the same time. This really makes sense!!

---

29 | Teach It

Course	U.S. History, U.S. Government, World History / Civilization, Economics, Geography, English Composition, Literature, Biology, Chemistry, Earth Science, Life Science, Physics, Health, Discrete Math, Algebra, Geometry, Calculus, Trigonometry, Statistics, Foreign Language, Art History, Art Appreciation, Online Courses, Career Education
Goal	To learn by teaching
Materials needed	Class notes, test information, handouts, white board, (optional) and other material that needs to be learned for a test.
Student comments	*"I use this strategy with my whiteboard. It's fun and I learn a lot."*
Professor comments	*"The strategy is really good because the student is actively engaged...I know they learn more when they have to teach the material".*
Lesson duration	40 – 60 minutes
Finished product to be graded	a copy of your lesson

Why do I need to learn this?

One of the best ways to learn anything is to teach it to someone else. Students like being the teacher. They prepare a lesson and then "Teach It". This strategy involves selecting the material, writing about it, and then delivering it. It is an active strategy and involves reading, writing, and speaking.

Getting Ready for the Activity

1. Assemble class notes and corresponding textbook material.

The Activity

2. Prepare a 10-15 minute lesson and "give" it to either a friend, family member, your class or to yourself.

Home Learning

Review your notes by explaining the material out loud in the same way your instructor presented the information.

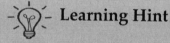 **Learning Hint**

Being able to teach something to someone else is a good indication of whether or not you know the information.

30 | Visual-Text Connection

Course	U.S. History, U.S. Government, World History / Civilization, Economics, Geography, Literature, Biology, Chemistry, Earth Science, Life Science, Physics, Physical Education, Health, Art History, Art Appreciation, Online Courses, Career Education
Goal	To connect visual information with the written explanation from the textbook
Materials needed	Textbook and other reference material that has visual information, pencil and pen
Student comments	*"I never used to look at the visual material. Now I've learned that connecting the visuals with the written explanation helps me understand what I'm supposed to learn."*
Professor comments	*"Many students never look at the charts, graphs, diagrams and other visual material which are there to clarify the text. This is an excellent strategy!"*
Lesson duration	Approximately 15 minutes per each visual
Finished product to be graded	Using your textbook, show your instructor how you connected the visual / graphic with the written information.

Why do I need to learn this?

"Visual-Text Connection" (VTC is a study strategy that significantly enhances learning visual / graphic information. It "connects" the visual / graphic to the written information. Most textbooks have diagrams and accompanying written explanations. For example, in most biology courses, students must learn the steps of cell division called meiosis. There is a diagram which illustrates each stage and also a written explanation. "Visual-Text Connection" is a "short cut" for learning the name of all the stages and functions and is especially helpful for a picture label test.

Getting Ready for the Activity

1. Identify a visual/graphic you want to learn about.
2. Find the corresponding information from the text which explains the visual/graphic.

The Activity

3. Connect the written information from the text to the visual/graphic in the text by drawing a line from the text to the visual/graphic.
4. When reviewing, study both the visual/graphic and the connecting explanation from the text.

Home Learning

Use this strategy for all visual/graphic material in the text. Test yourself by making sure you can reproduce and explain all parts of the visual/graphic from memory.

 Learning Hint

Use colored pencils to color code your connecting lines. Visual/graphic material is included to facilitate learning. Often it is more efficient to spend more time studying the visual/graphic than reading about it.

Bonus Chapter

Eight Bonus Strategies-- these are too good to miss!

During the first year of college you will take English and humanity classes as well as mathematic classes. These are required courses and unfortunately rank as the top college classes that generate failing grades. The bonus chapter is designed to help you through these courses.

The first group of four BONUS Strategies that are "too good to miss" are in Mathematics:

> Back-Up System Modified for Math
> Bank Deposits
> Camera Roll
> Validity Web

4 Bonus Strategies for Math
Back-Up System Modified for Mathematics

Course	Discrete Math, Algebra, Geometry, Calculus, Trigonometry, Probability/Statistics
Goal	To keep up-to-date with mathematics class notes and textbook
Materials needed	Journal/notebook, class notes, old tests, and pencil
Student comments	*"'Back-Up System' is OK but it takes a lot of discipline to do it before every math class. But, when I do it, my grades definitely improve."*
Instructor comments	*"I try to impress upon my students two extremely and basic ways to become good in math---practice and repetition. 'Back-Up System' fulfills both of these principles."*
Lesson Duration	20-30 minutes before each math class
Finished product to be graded	Your journal/notebook which has the entries, notes, formulas, terms, and problems used in each math review session before class

Why do I need to learn this?

The "Back-Up System" is one of the best ways to review because the material stays fresh in your mind and safeguards against forgetting. Here is how it works: Suppose you had a Monday, Wednesday, and Friday math class. Before each Monday class you will read over the notes from the last class. *Then you will go back and review all the previous notes beginning with the first class. You will be reviewing at least three times a week so the material will be in your long-term memory. Your math formulas will be memorized effortlessly and be available when you need them for the test.*

Getting Ready for the Activity

1. Schedule 20-30 minutes before each math class for review.
2. Have all of your past math class notes and math textbook available to review before your next math class.

The Activity

3. Twenty to thirty minutes before your math class begins, review the previous class notes.
4. Find the section in the textbook that explains the concept (problem) and that has practice problems and read carefully.
5. Use your notes and begin reviewing starting with the first class to the present class.
6. Use your journal/notebook to keep a running account of each review session by writing the date, a few notes, important formulas, terms/definitions, and any important information you think you should know. Use your journal/notebook to rework the demonstration problems.

Home Learning

Give yourself a self-test by writing each formula from memory and solving the math problems from class and the practice problems from the textbook.

 Learning Hint

If class information is reviewed often, it will be easy to retrieve when taking a test. If the "Back-Up System for Mathematics" is used two or three times a week, a student will not have to "cram" for a test the night before an exam.

Bank Deposits

Course	Discrete Math, Algebra, Geometry, Calculus, Trigonometry, Probability/Statistics
Goal	To remember formulas and specific operations needed during math quizzes and tests.
Materials needed	Math textbook, class notes, old tests, homework problems, notebook, calculator, pencil
Student comments	*"I used to be so nervous before math tests. Now I don't get so stressed because I write all the important formulas on the back of the test."*
Professor comments	*"It's a shame to miss a math problem because a student couldn't remember a formula."*
Lesson duration	Time will vary according to the number of formulas to be memorized.
Finished product to be graded	Go over returned test with teacher. Explain how Bank Deposits related to test questions. Bring all homework problems to show teacher that you have memorized the formulas and are able to write them from memory.

Why do I need to learn this?

Bank Deposits makes certain you remember everything you studied. Just as we make money deposits in the bank for safe keeping, we write our formulas on the back of the test (for safe keeping) so we can use when we need them during the test.

Getting Ready for the Activity

1. One week before a math exam, use your class notes and textbook and select all the formulas you need to know.

The Activity

2. Write each formula in a special section of your notebook and make a few notes about how and why the formula should be used.

3. Rework all the demonstration problems that relate to the formulas that will be on your test or quiz. Make sure you do the problems with the book closed and then check that your answer and procedure matches the steps in the textbook.

4. Rework the homework problems that gave you trouble and that you missed on the practice exercises. Do this regardless of whether or not you receive credit for doing the homework.

5. Make sure you are doing all of your homework when assigned. During class ask questions about homework problems. Do not wait until the end of the marking period or the day before the exam to ask questions.

6. Make a bank number deposit. With a pencil or pen, write down all the formulas and procedures that you studied the night before. Write these on the back of the test or quiz as soon as it is handed to you.

7. Read through the test or quiz quickly and thoroughly.

8. Begin by answering only the questions that you know you will get correct. Circle the questions that you skip.

9. Use your bank number deposits from the back to help answer your questions.

10. Watch the clock. Develop a time line that gets you through all the problems on time.

11.   Use all the time. Check to make sure you have answered all the questions.

Home Learning

Make a mock test. On the back of the mock test, write all the formulas you have been memorizing. Practice taking the test in the time frame that you will have in class. Check your answers to see if your bank number deposits are sufficient.

> ### Learning Hint
> When reading or studying, always make sure to mark or indicate any formulas, date, process, or other information that you intend to remember. Remember, that in almost every class there is going to be information that has to be memorized. It's up to you to make sure you have selected that information!!

Camera Roll

Course	U.S. History, U.S. Government, World History / Civilization, Economics, Geography, English Composition, Literature, Biology, Chemistry, Earth Science, Life Science, Physics, Physical Education, Health, ROTC, Discrete Math, Algebra, Geometry, Calculus, Trigonometry, Statistics, Foreign Language, Art History, Art Appreciation, Band, Music, Online Courses, Career Education
Goal	To learn information from photos from the textbook
Materials needed	Textbook and smart phone
Student comments	*"I never learned much from reading my math textbook until I started using 'Camera Roll'. I learn a lot because I take pictures of the formulas and other things I should memorize for math. Whenever I have a few minutes, I go to my "Camera Roll" and look at all the pictures I have about math. I know this strategy has helped me a lot."*
Instructor comments	*"'Camera Roll' is great for visual learners. Most students like to take fun pictures from the textbook. I find students willingly do this because they like anything that has do with their phone! Although I recommend it for math, it is a great strategy for most courses but I especially like it for math because of all the graphic/visual information found in a math textbook."*
Lesson Duration	Time will vary
Finished product to be graded	Have student meet with the instructor to show all the photos that were taken from the math textbook and also the notebook. Ask students to explain "purpose of the photo "and the most important thing learned from the photo".

Why do I need to learn this?

Many students overlook the visual/graphic information from a textbook. They fail to realize that photos, charts, graphs, drawings, problems, and formulas can often explain important information in a more comprehensible way than words.

Getting Ready for the Activity

1. Select a chapter from a textbook.
2. Tell students to bring a cell phone, textbook, and notebook to the next class.

The Activity

3. Instruct students to take a photo of each chart, graph, photo, drawing and any other visual/graphic material from the selected chapter in a math textbook. Go to Camera Roll. Read the caption for each photo and read the section in the textbook that gives the purpose and explanation of the photo.
4. Write in the notebook (1) the purpose of each photo and (2) the important "thing" I learned from the photo.

Home Learning

For homework, review "Camera Roll" and write a question and answer that a teacher might ask about each photo. Collect the questions and answers from the students and give a "mock quiz" for review.

 Learning Hint
Encourage students to use 'Camera Roll' in all classes. Remind them that they will always have something to study since they are never without their phone!

Validity Web

Course	Discrete Math, Algebra, Geometry, Calculus, Trigonometry, Statistics,
Goal	To understand math word problems
Materials needed	Math, Algebra, Geometry, Calculus, Trigonometry, or Statistics textbook.
Student comments	*"The hardest part of algebra is to understand the word problem and write out the equation. I always ask how many word problems will be on the test, then I shiver at the thought. Bummer!"*
Instructor comments	*"I teach algebra, geometry and sometimes calculus. Most students cannot master word problems. Many times I feel sad when I include them on tests because I know it is these problems that will lower test scores."*
Lesson Duration	One hour
Finished product to be graded	Turn in the completed "Validity Web" from a word problem from any mathematic book. Include a copy of the word problem.

Why do I need to learn this?

A portion of the core curriculum includes taking and passing a minimum of six hours of math and algebra. Many students "stumble" on the word problems that resemble the equations which they know how to do. This strategy will help you make sense of the word problems you must solve.

Getting Ready for the Activity

1. You will probably want to do this exercise with a math textbook.
2. Make sure you have uninterrupted time to follow the steps on the practice exercise below. Set aside about one hour for the entire exercise.
3. For this exercise you will need a pencil with an eraser. Also make sure you leave the validity web matrix below unmarked so you can have it for a master.
4. Make sure the word problems have the level of equation you know how to solve.

The Activity

5. In order to do this strategy of solving word problems, you will be asked to write valid and invalid information on the validity web sheet in the appropriate boxes. Valid information is relevant and invalid information is irrelevant. You will be also asked to find a similar problem in your textbook and write the steps and equation in the Sample Problem box on the validity web sheet.
6. Word problem: Harry Cook is 50 years old and is very tall. He loves to eat 5 pieces of fruit a day to keep his blood pressure down. Also, he runs five miles per day for exercise. Allen Cook is 25 years younger and Harry Cook is twice the age of Allen Cook. Allen Cook is much taller than Harry and eats junk food. Allen Cook can only run ½ mile when exercising. How old is Allen Cook?
7. Go to the Validity Web Sheet. In the middle circle write ONLY the question the word problem is asking. This was done for you on page 85.

8.   Next examine the two boxes on each side of the circle. One is labeled valid which is full of information you need to answer the questions. The other is labeled invalid which is information not needed to answer the question.

9.   Go line by line and place the information in the correct box- valid or invalid. Again the sample was done for you.

10. Now, in the solution box let's assign Allen Cook's age the letter X. We picked Allen Cook's age because it is the question in the word problem. His age is what we are looking to solve. He is in the circle box.

11. In the valid box we placed Harry A. Cook I is 50 years old. We also placed that Harry Cook is twice the age of Allen Cook. In the invalid box we placed that Harry Cook runs 5 miles per day, and eats fruit. We also placed in the invalid box that Allen Cook is taller than Harry Cook, runs ½ mile per day and eats junk food.

12. Now, look in your textbook and write in the sample problem box a similar problem to help guide you.

     12. So you will see in the solution box the equation is

          X= 50 - 25
          X=25

     1.   X = 25. Allen Cook is 25 years old.

13. Now you do this problem on the validity chart. You have five red apples in your refrigerator. You need six more to make an apple pie. You go to the store and buy twice as many red apples you have in the refrigerator plus one, three oranges and ½ pound of cherries. How many red apples do you have in total when you get home?

Hint: (1) Write the question you are trying to find out in the circle.
(2) Make sure you list the valid information and the invalid information in the
appropriate boxes. Find a sample problem in your text(3) Using only the
valid information, write your equation and solve for X. (4) Remember X is
what the questions is asking you to find out.

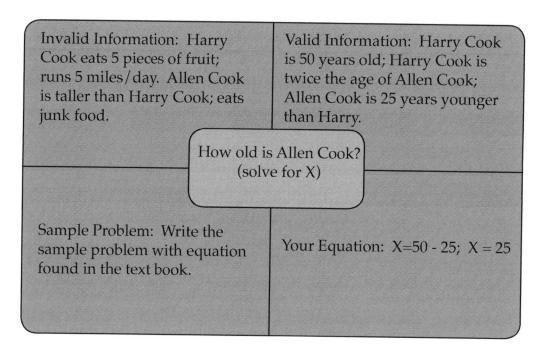

Invalid Information: Harry
Cook eats 5 pieces of fruit;
runs 5 miles/day. Allen Cook
is taller than Harry Cook; eats
junk food.

Valid Information: Harry Cook
is 50 years old; Harry Cook is
twice the age of Allen Cook;
Allen Cook is 25 years younger
than Harry.

How old is Allen Cook?
(solve for X)

Sample Problem: Write the
sample problem with equation
found in the text book.

Your Equation: $X = 50 - 25$; $X = 25$

Home Learning
Write a word problem and then fill out the Validity Web using your word
problem. Be ready to share your problem with the class.

Extension
Go to your math or algebra text. Fill out the Validity chart with one of
the word problems. Make sure you write out the word problem and text
it came from on your Validity Web.

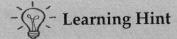 **Learning Hint**

1. Read the word problem carefully. Look for valid and invalid information.

2. The question in the word problem will always be what you are ultimately looking for. Assign the question a variable such as X.

3. Always rewrite the question. When using a validity web always rewrite the question in the circle of the web.

4. Be sure to separate valid (relevant) information and invalid (irrelevant) information.

5. Using the valid information only, write your equation.

Bonus Chapter

The second group of four Bonus Strategies
that are "too good to miss" are for the required
English and Humanities classes.

Check the Facts

Patterns of Organization

Prepositions and Transitions

Writing Around the Table

Check the Facts

Course	U.S. History, U.S. Government, World History / Civilization, Economics, Geography, English Composition, Literature, Biology, Chemistry, Earth Science, Life Science, Physics, Physical Education, Health, Art History, Art Appreciation, Online Courses, Career Education
Goal	To learn both sides of a history event or political issue
Materials needed	Internet, reliable resources
Student comments	*" I have learned not to be so gullible and to believe everything I see and hear. I have also learned that there are at least two sides to most things."*
Professor comments	*"I encourage students to think for themselves and not to take everything at face value."*
Lesson duration	40 – 60 minutes.
Finished product to be graded	Make a copy of your notes that show the fact from the textbook and the references used to "check the fact". Be sure to cite any conflicts regarding discrepancies, omissions, and bias.

Why do I need to learn this?

"Check the Facts" is a strategy that requires readers to examine text material through analytical analysis. Many students memorize important facts when studying history and political science. However, on the college level, professors expect you to think critically about your topic's main ideas in reference to bias and validity. Students need to know both sides of an argument. This strategy offers an easy way to review, study, and learn information from opposing sides. It will help you become a better student when thinking critically about issues and events in other classes.

Getting Ready for the Activity

1. Choose a content textbook from one of your history classes.
2. Go to the next assigned chapter. If there is a chapter that needs rereading for an impending test, then use that chapter. The course syllabus can be consulted in making a decision on what chapter to use.
3. Make sure you have taken your lecture notes in a T fashion.

The Activity

4. Begin reviewing your notes that are on the left side of the T. The right hand side of the T should be blank.
5. Use a fact reliable resources or a checking website to confirm or take issue. Some common fact checking websites are Snopes, FactCheck.org, WhoWhatWhen, PolitiFACT, and Buzzfeed.
6. Use the right side of the T to write a different or opposing point of view.

Home Learning

Study your T notes for tests and quizzes. Learning both sides of an issue is a good way to prepare for essay exams.

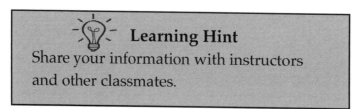

Learning Hint

Share your information with instructors and other classmates.

Patterns of Organization

Course	U.S. History, U.S. Government, World History / Civilization, Economics, Geography, English Composition, Literature, Biology, Chemistry, Earth Science, Life Science, Physics, Physical Education, Health Art History, Art Appreciation, Online Courses, Career Education
Goal	To learn how to identify patterns of organization in textbooks and in lectures
Materials needed	Content textbook, pencil, highlighter, paper
Student comments	*" I never realized that my professors used patterns of organization for their lectures. It's really interesting to try to figure out what pattern they used for their lectures."*
Professor comments	*"I think 'Pattern of Organization' is a good strategy to teach but I think there are two really good benefits: (1) it helps students become better writers and (2) it helps students when trying to recall the information."*
Lesson duration	one class session
Finished product to be graded	Show your instructor the 15 paragraphs in your textbook with the pattern of organization written next to it.

Why do I need to learn this?

Comprehending and remembering information from textbooks and lectures can be challenging. However, if the material is well-organized, it becomes easier to understand. Being able to detect the pattern that was used to organize the material makes it easier to grasp the meaning and to predict forthcoming information. If someone can process information in the same way the author or lecture organized the information, he or she is likely to understand, remember, and retrieve the information when it is needed for a test.

Getting Ready for the Activity

1. Review the nine patterns of organization and signal words associated with each pattern.

Patterns that catalogue information

Patterns of Organization	Signal Words
Time-Order: The Time-Order Pattern, also Known as the Chronological pattern, presents Items in a sequence, chronological order, or the order in which they occurred.	stages, steps, previously, first, second, third, until, at last, before, after, next, later, following, during
Spatial/Place: The Spatial pattern identifies the location or whereabouts of an object. This pattern helps the reader use words to form visual locations.	above, over, under, nearby, around, next to, beside, below, behind, outside, in front of, north, south, east, west

Summary: The Summary pattern condenses major points and significant details into a brief version of the original piece.

finally, in brief, overall, hence, to conclude, in summary

Patterns that give information

Patterns of Organization	Signal Words
Example: The Example pattern uses examples explain, clarify, and/or illustrate an idea or concept.	specifically, for example, to that is, for instance, such as, to illustrate, Including, to show, to demonstrate
Definition: The Definition pattern defines the specialized vocabulary, ideas, terms, and concepts which are often clarified with examples and restatements.	is defined as, is called, means, refers to, a term, concept to be described, features
Description: The Description pattern describes or illustrates the characteristics of a person, place, or thing. Usually a "picture" of the thing is created.	to describe, features, looks like, can be described

Patterns that analyze

Patterns of Organization	Signal Words
Classification/Division/Topic List: The Classification/Division/Topic List pattern used with topics or concepts which have several categories or parts. information is divided into groups and then each one is explained.	aspects, properties, divided into, groups, is parts, categories, elements, types, features, characteristics, divisions, kinds, styles
Cause-Effect: The Cause-Effect pattern is used to show that something happened caused an effect on something else. This pattern usually involves the how, why, consequences, and results.	since, thus, as a result, because, leads to, which consequently, hence, therefore, due to, accordingly, if....then
Comparison/Contrast: The Compare/Contrast shows the similarities and differences between two things. The Comparison pattern shows how things are similar; the Contrast pattern shows how things are different.	as well as, similar, pattern different, than, instead, however, parallels, on the other hand, but, in the same way, like, alike, whereas, nevertheless

The Activity

2. Refer to the Table of Contents in the textbook. Determine the overall pattern of organization the author used in this book.

3. Determine the pattern of organization used for the next assigned chapter.

4. Choose 15 paragraphs in the chapter. Read each one and decide which pattern of
   Organization was used: Time-Order, Spatial/Place, Summary, Example, Definition, Description, Classification/Division/Topic List, Cause-Effect, Comparison/Contrast
   (Note that some paragraphs may use a combination of several paragraphs in one paragraph).

5. Write the name of the pattern or organization next to each paragraph.

Home Learning

Determine the pattern of organization used in the textbooks and lectures from your other courses.

Learning Hint

Before you begin a summary, essay, or other writing assignment, choose a pattern of organization to develop your information. Remember, that different pattern of organization may be used for individual patterns and another pattern used overall for the entire paper.

Transitions and Prepositions

Introduction: Transitions and Prepositions

"Transitions and Prepositions" is the "step by step" strategy that instructs students how transitions and prepositions are used to show relationships between and within sentences. The strategy lays the foundation as readers progress to more advanced reading material with more and more critical reading demands. Knowing how transitions and prepositions are used will help readers with the reading skills of Implied main ideas, Author's organizational pattern, Relationships within and between sentences, Authors's purpose, Tone, Fact and Opinion, Drawing Conclusions, and Inferences.

Course:	English, Humanities, any course that requires written assignments
Goal:	To learn how transitions and prepositions are used with implicit and critical thinking reading material
Student Comments:	*My teachers sometimes mark my sentences as fragments and comma splices. I even had one teacher tell me that this "is not a complete thought."*
Professor Comments:	*We may be in college, but my students have trouble with compound and complex sentences and punctuation. This is not tolerated at this level.*
Material:	English handbook.
Time duration:	one class period
Finish product to be graded:	Completion of the 11 "Step by Step Strategy"

Why do I need to learn this?

At times prepositions can be confusing. They are usually the words that simply show relationships within and between sentences. Using the wrong preposition can cause confusion or completely change the meaning of the sentence.

How do I learn this strategy?

Complete Steps 1-11

1.   Memorize the most commonly used prepositions in the English language.

aboard	about	above	across	after
against	along	amid	among	around
as	at	before	behind	below
beneath	beside	between	beyond	but
by	concerning	considering	despite	down
during	except	excluding	following	for
from	in	inside	into	like
minus	near	of	off	on
onto	opposite	out	outside	over
past	per	plus	regarding	round
save	since	than	through	throughout
till	to	toward	under	underneath
until	up	upon	versus	via
with	within	without		

2.   Now that you have memorized all these propositions, write them on the space provided below without looking at the list. See how many you have. Did you remember all of them?

My List of Prepositions

_____
_____
_____
_____
_____
_____
_____
_____

If you remembered 50-68 excellent
                            40-49 good
                            30-39 fair
Less than 30 prepositions   Better do this exercise again!

3.   Now memorize the most commonly used prepositional phrases in the English language.

according to	along with	apart from
as a matter of fact	as regards	as to
because of	by means of	by reason of
by way of	due to	except for
in addition to	in brief	in back of
in case of	in conclusion	in front of
in lieu of	in like manner	in other words

in place of	in regard to	in spite of
reference to	instead of	on account of
on the other hand	on the contrary	on top of
out of	up to	with regard to
with respect to		

4.   Now that you rememorized all these prepositional phrases, write them on the space below without looking at the list. See how many you can remember. Did you remember all of them?

My list of prepositional phrases:

_____

_____

_____

_____

_____

_____

_____

_____

_____

_____

_____

_____

> If you remembered 28 prepositional phrases: excellent
> If you remembered 20 prepositional phrases: good
> If you remembered less than 20 prepositional phrases:
> Better do the exercise again!

The Activity

5.   For each of the blank spaces, choose a different preposition that shows a different position for the airplane. Use your list of prepositions (#1)
a.   The airplane flew _____ the clouds.
b.   The airplane flew _____ the clouds.
c.   The airplane flew _____ the clouds.

Discuss your answers with your classmates. See how many different prepositions give different meanings to the sentence.

6.   Now let's do the same thing but from a different approach. Read the sentences below. Notice the underlined words in the sentences. Can you recognize the different relationships in the sentences?
a.   The dog ran <u>around</u> the house.
b.   The dog ran <u>into</u> the house.
c.   The dog ran <u>behind</u> the house.
d.   The dog ran <u>past</u> the house.

With your classmates, discuss the different meanings each preposition gives.

7.   Now let's look at related usage when it comes to prepositions.

•   The preposition must indicate the correct relationship between parts of the sentences and between two or more sentences.

•   **At** and **To**
At is used to indicate that the person or thing is already there.
To is used to indicate that the person or thing is going there.
Example: Jean is at home (Not "to" home.)
            Francis is running to school.

- **Between** and **Among**

Between is used in speaking of *two*.

Among is used in speaking of *more than two*.

Example: The tent was pitched *between* the two pines.

        The stream would its way *among* many trees.

- *In* and *Into*

In is used to indicate that the person or thing is there.

Into is used to suggest a movement to get there.

Example: The letter is *in* the box.

        The frog jumped *into* the pond.

- **Off of**

Off of should not be used for *off or from*.

Example: The baby fell *off* the bed. (used correctly)

        They took it *from* her. (used correctly)

- **Different**

The adjective *different* should be followed by the preposition ***from*** and not the preposition ***than***.

Example: This key is different *than* mine. (INCORRECT)

        This key is different *from* mine. (CORRECT)

- **Unnecessary propositions**

Avoid using an unnecessary preposition.

Example: I wanted *for* my mother to come. (POOR)

        I wanted my mother to come. (IMPROVED)

- **In back of** versus **behind**

Do not use the expression *in back of* for behind.

In back of the house stood a big apple tree. (POOR)

Behind the house stood a big apple tree. (IMPROVED)

- **Object of the preposition**

A preposition is always followed by a noun or pronoun. This noun or pronoun is called the object of the preposition. When it is a pronoun, use the pronoun **me**, **not I** as the object of a preposition.

Example: (noun): The cake is for Jose. ("for" is the preposition and "Jose" is the noun)

Example: (pronoun): He gave gifts to *me*.

He gave gifts *to my sister and me.*

They talked *about me.*

They talked about *Francis and me.*

- **Prepositional Phrase**

A prepositional phrase is the preposition and the object of the preposition together.

Example: The clean clothes are *in the dryer.*

I went *into the house.*

- **Prepositional Usage**

Prepositions cannot end a sentence. This is because a preposition is always followed by a noun or pronoun.

Example: I turned the DVD on. (INCORRECT)

I turned on the DVD (CORRECT)

8.   Circle the correct word in each parenthesis. Use the rules listed on the previous pages to help you.

a.   Alice was not (at, to) school yesterday.

b.   I hoped (to win, for to win).

c.   The money will be divided (between, among) the four sons.

d.   We were (to, at) that place several times.

e.   There was an alliance (between, among) the five nations.

f.   I have some of those bushes (at, to) home.

g.   We should not ask a favor (from, off or) her.

h.   Please go (in, into) the library and stay (in, into) that room till noon.

i.   I was not (at, to) home last week.

j.   They took the blanket (off of, off) the horse.

k.   William is different (than, from) his brother.

l.   Early this morning my father was (at, to) the farm.

m.   The boys plunged quickly (into, in) the cool water.

n.   I have been (in, into) the house for an hour.

o.   Make the new poster different (from, than) the old one.

p.   She took the blanket (off of, off) the front seat for (me, I).

q.   I hope they don't leave without Allen and (I, me).

r.   (In, On) the theater, she sat with Jimmy and (I, me).

9. Read these sentences and fill in each blank with the proper preposition from the list of prepositions (pg. 96)

a. _____the two trees stood a quaint stone house.

b. The morning's catch was divided _____the five boys.

c. Don't stay_____ home all day.

d. Did you find your sister _____school.

e. My plan for a party is different _____yours.

f. _____the four girls there was a feeling of rivalry.

g. We bought this magazine _____Mr. Fisher.

h. Is the doctor _____at home?

i. I found him _____school.

j. I want one different _____his.

k. That day I was _____my brother's house.

l. Who took the cookies _____the pantry shelf?

m. If the men and women cannot agree, they must settle the difficulty _____ themselves.

10. Prepositional phrases. Circle the prepositional phrases in the sentences below.

a. The piece of clear glass shone like new silver.

b. The boys jumped into the pile of hay.

c. The heavy curtains at the front of the window were soiled and torn.

d. In the theater, she sat next to my father and me.

e. He divided the money between Bill and me.

f. The life of a butterfly is short.

g. A blast of cold air stung their faces.

103

h. The lines of this play are well-written.

i. The newspapers were filled with pictures of the team.

j. Andy is the boy without a sweater.

k. The present was from Joey and me.

l. Everyone went home with Bobby and me.

11. **The following exercise shows *Relationships within Sentences***

Directions: Write your own sentences with the prepositional phrases given using the relationships indicated. Share with your classmates.

a. Relationship: addition   Prepositional phrase: along with Tommy

Your sentence: _____

b. Relationship: clarification   Prepositional phrase: in other words

Your sentence: _____

c. Relationship: comparison   Prepositional phrase: in like manner

Your sentence: _____

d. Relationship: contrast   Prepositional phrase: on the other hand

Your sentence: _____

e. Relationship: example   Prepositional phrase: for instance

Your sentence: _____

Writing Around the Table

Course:	English, Literature, Humanities, First Year Experience, Analytical Analysis
Goal:	Help students write with unity, coherence, support and grammar skills
Materials:	writing paper, pen or pencil, English Handbook, picture
Student Comments:	*This activity was fun because I had a chance to work with my classmates and create a good essay.*
Professor Comments:	*This activity helped students learn from each other. Each students was responsible for his or her particular part of the essay, but hey had support from classmates in the group.*
Lesson Duration:	1 ½ hours
Finish Product to Be Graded:	Finished Essay

Goals:

To provide writing practice to students through having them experience writing in different phrases: introduction, body, conclusion and editor.

To foster critical thinking about one's own writing as well as others. To transfer reading skills studied into written practice.

Why do I need to learn this?

This practice will give you an insight into your own writing abilities through viewing your classmates. Innocent writing mistakes of group members such as weak thesis statements and supporting paragraphs will become extremely evident to you because it will make your task of continuing the essay difficult to manage. As a result, you will become more aware of your own writing strengths and weaknesses. But more importantly, this task will sharpen your written communicative and editing skills.

Getting Ready for the Activity

1. Divide the class into groups of 5-6 members.
2. Ask each group member to bring a picture from a magazine that will sparkle interest for writing.
3. Ask group members to sit together, preferably at a round table.
4. Each group member must have a copy of the Writing Around the Table Graphic Organizer found on page 111.
5. Each group member must have a pencil with a good eraser for writing the essay and a pen for editing.

The Activity

6. Using the picture, each group member must write an introduction to a story/essay that supports the picture. Remember to write the introduction on the Writing Around the Table Graphic Organizer. Write with a pencil!
   Take ten minutes to write your introduction. Keep in mind your professor's lecture on strong introductions. Also, take two minutes and review the Learning Hint box found at the bottom of the next page. Do not forget to write your first name on the author line on the introduction paragraph. After completing the introduction, each group member must pass the picture and his/her introduction to the right.
7. Upon receiving the new introduction and picture, write your name on the author line next to the first paragraph. Scan through the Learning Hint box again paying careful attention to all the information provided. Then, each member must read silently the introduction, study the picture and continue the story writing only

the first paragraph. Again remember your professor's lectures on supporting the thesis of an essay, following the plan of development implied or explicitly written in the introduction, and developing a strong supporting paragraph with a topic sentence and supporting details. A good strategy is to think of the main idea exercises and supporting detail exercises found in your reading text. Use these exercises and structure patterns as a model. The first paragraph should take about ten minutes to write. After completing the first paragraph, pass the graphic organizer and picture to the write.

8. Upon receiving the picture, introduction and first paragraph, each member must read silently the introduction and first paragraph, study the picture and continue the story writing only the second paragraph. In writing the second paragraph, use the same skills and tactics employed to write the first paragraph! Budget ten minutes to write and do not forget to sign your name on the author line next to the second paragraph. Again, after completing the paragraph, each member must pass the graphic organizer and picture to the right.

9. Upon receiving the picture, introduction and first and second paragraphs, each member must read the story silently, study the picture and continue the story writing only the third paragraph. Follow the same procedure used in paragraphs one and two. Take ten minutes. Sign your name on the author's line. Again, after completing the paragraph, each member must pass the graphic organizer and picture to the right.

10. Now write the conclusion. Carefully read the introduction and body of the essay. Then reread the Learning Hints on conclusions and think about the drawing conclusion exercises in your reading text. Make good use of all this information. Take ten minutes and sign your name on the author's line. Then pass the graphic organizer to the right for editing.

11. Edit with a pen. Scan through the Editor's section in the Learning Hints. Then carefully read the entire essay before marking. Take your time reading! Then reread the essay with the intent to make changes as necessary. Check for (1) sentence structure (2) punctuation (3)

word choice (4) a strong thesis statement (5) implied or stated plan of development in the introduction (6) overall strong introduction (7) topic sentences and supporting details for each paragraph (8) discussion in each of the three points as outlined in the introduction- one point per paragraph- and (9) a strong conclusion that does not add additional information to the plain of discussion but ventures beyond a simple summary of the facts. Feel free to make changes within the text as well as write editor's notes. Turn in the edited version to the professor.

Home Learning

Instead of turning in the edited graphic organizer, take the essay home and type it with the corrections. Submit the marked-up draft (graphic organizer) and the final typed version the next class period.

Extension

Show pictures and read the essay to the class. Be prepared to tell the class any techniques or style you learned from your group member as well as any changes you plan to employ in your writing.

-💡-Learning Hint

Writing	Reading
Introduction- Although the thesis statement can appear anywhere in the introductory paragraph, it is usually found near the beginning. Most writers begin their introductory paragraphs with 1-3 sentences introducing the topic and trying to create interest, followed by a thesis statement that positions the paper and finished with a purpose and/or plan of development statement(s).	**Introduction-** The thesis statement can be located towards the beginning, middle or end of the introductory paragraph. It is usually stated but can be implied. Most introductory paragraphs offer the reader a purpose statement and plan of development. Note in your reading text the different types of purposes.

The introduction is a very important task of writing an essay. Create an interesting lead into the topic. Make sure your topic is clear and you give your topic direction. Create a strong and appealing thesis sentence. Your other writers terrible need this to perform their task. Be concise and clear. Remember to state or imply three major areas (plan of development) that will give direction to the thesis and lead the discussion.

Writing	Reading
Body- Do not forget to begin your paragraphs with a transitional word or statement; this will help you smoothly move from one paragraph to another. This statement should be followed by a topic sentence and then major and minor supporting details. Remember each paragraph of the body should support the thesis statement and follow the purpose and plan of development as stated or implied in the introduction.	**Body-** You studied the body of a paragraph when you answered supporting detail questions. Remember in your exercises you identified major and minor supporting details. You also answered questions concerning if the minor supporting details were supporting the topic sentence or the major supporting detail. You also studied the different types of relationships between and within sentences. Use the key words in relationships to help you make a smooth transition.

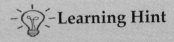 **Learning Hint**

Writing   Reading

Each paragraph in the body should discuss one the three points or ideas identified in the introduction's plan of development. While writing, keep in mind the purpose.

Conclusion- Your conclusion should rehash the points brought out in the essay. However venture a little further and think about including predictions, outcomes, call for action or any other comment that does not add any additional information.	**Conclusion-** In your reading text, when drawing a conclusion you were asked to choose the most logical answer-outcome, prediction, or action- according to the information in the introduction and body. As a reader, the exercise was assessing your ability to choose the most logical ending.

Editor: Check for sentence structure, punctuation, and essay organization and coherence throughout the essay.

Writing Around the Table Graphic Outline

Introduction
By _____

_____
_____
_____
_____
_____
_____
_____

Body-Paragraph I
By _____

_____
_____
_____
_____
_____
_____
_____

Body Paragraph II
By _____

_____
_____
_____
_____
_____
_____

Body Paragraph III
By_____

_____
_____
_____
_____
_____
_____
_____

Body Paragraph IV
By_____

_____

_____

_____

_____

_____

_____

_____

_____

Conclusion
By_____

_____

_____

_____

_____

_____

_____

_____

_____

Editor's notes

_____

_____

_____

_____

_____

_____

_____

_____

Answer Key

Transitions and Prepositions

8. (page 102)

a at

b. to win

c. among

d. at

e. among

f. at

g. from

h. into, in

i. at

j. off

k. from

l. at

m. into

n. in

o. from

p. off, me

q. me

r. in, me

9. (page 103)

a. Between

b. among

c. at

d. at

e. from

f. Among

g. from

h. still

i. at

j. from

k. at

l. from

m. between

10. (page 103)

a. of clear glass

b. into the pile, of hay

c. at the front, of the window

d. to my father and me

e. between Bill and me

f. of a butterfly

g. of cold air

h. of this play

i. with pictures, of the team

j without a sweater

k. from Joey and me

l. with Bobby and me

11. (page 104)

Answers vary

About the Authors

Patsy Trand, Ph.D., is a faculty member of Florida International University and the former administrator of the FIU Reading and Learning Lab. Dr. Trand teaches undergraduate, honors, and graduate courses for the FIU School of Arts and Sciences. She is committed to passing on her wealth of knowledge and experience to help high school and college students reach their academic goals. She has authored many articles and has presented at many national and international conferences.

Kay Lopate, Ph.D., is a Professor Emeritus from the University of Miami, Miami, Florida where she co-founded the Reading and Study Skills Center and taught for the School of Education. Her special interests are preparing PreMed students for medical school and helping undergraduates acquire advanced reading ability to succeed in the demands of mastering college level texts.

Dear Students,

In our long careers as professors at two major universities we have always come to the same two conclusions:

A college education is based on reading

and

Students with high levels of reading comprehension performed well in their classes and went on to earn their college degree.

"The 30 Amazing Reading and Learning Strategies for College Students", based on our conclusions, is the collection of reading and learning strategies that we have developed and used with undergraduate and graduate students. In working with our students we have always emphasized that

"It doesn't matter what your reading level is now—what matters is what your reading level can become."

We believe that "The 30 Amazing Reading and Learning Strategies for College Students" will be a key factor that will help you **"become the student you aspire to become"**.

We hope you enjoyed the book and begin to use the strategies. We wish you the best as you continue to reach your educational goals,
Kay Lopate, Ph.D. and Patsy Trand, Ph.D.

Made in the USA
Columbia, SC
26 August 2020